the new cabbage soup diet

the new cabbage soup diet

by
margaret danbrot

BLAKE

Published by Blake Publishing Ltd,
3 Bramber Court, 2 Bramber Road,
London W14 9PB, England

First published in the UK in 2000

ISBN 1 85782 410 5

British Library Cataloguing-in-Publication Data:
A catalogue record for this book is available
from the British Library.

Typeset by t2

Printed in Great Britain by
Creative Print and Design (Wales),
Ebbw Vale, Gwent.

3 5 7 9 10 8 6 4

important note to readers

The reader should consult his or her doctor before beginning this or any other diet. Consulting one's doctor is particularly important if one is suffering from any illness or on any medication. All readers, however, should speak with their doctors before starting this diet to be sure it is appropriate for them.

The New Cabbage Soup Diet is not appropriate for long-term use. It is not intended as a substitute for good long-term eating habits. The diet may be used for up to a week, but after a week the reader should switch to a normal nutritionally-balanced diet for at least two weeks before returning to the New Cabbage Soup Diet. The reader should not use the New Cabbage Soup Diet too frequently, even with two-week or longer intervals in between uses.

Under no circumstances is the diet appropriate for children or adolescents.

conversion table

Dry Measures
1 cup is equal to 8 oz

Liquid Measures
1 cup is equal to 8 fl oz

contents

'The New Cabbage Soup Diet really works. I lost 9½ pounds in the first week and now feel terrific!'
Jack Nicklaus, world champion golfer

'It doesn't involve starving, you're never hungry, you don't feel deprived, you don't feel inclined to binge!'
Dr Miriam Stoppard

'It is the only diet I have ever stuck to. It's wonderful because it's not fiddly — the only thing you have to do is cook the soup. It's the best diet ever!'
Jilly Cooper

'There is no question that one loses seven to ten pounds in seven days!'
Chris Patten, former Governor of Hong Kong

what's all the excitement about?

Congratulations! You've just chosen the one diet book that will help you change your life forever. Because within these pages, you will find the secret to getting a huge jump-start on weight loss — ten pounds or more in a week! — as well as a plan for conquering any diet challenges you may encounter on the way to reaching your ideal weight. That jump-start, and that plan, of course, are what the Cabbage Soup Diet is all about.

As you'll soon see, the Cabbage Soup Diet is unlike any diet you've ever tried. In fact, it's so extraordinary that in telling you all about it, we're going to deviate from the classic diet book formula.

For instance, diet books usually begin with a lengthy pep talk to motivate the dieter and generate enthusiasm about the diet. There are dozens of reasons to feel upbeat and enthusiastic about the Cabbage Soup Diet. Firstly it's unique. In fact it's in a class by itself, unlike any other weight-loss plan you've heard or read about. It's different in structure, ingredients, and procedure, and these differences help make it supereffective at moving your body into quick weight-loss mode. It's easy to follow. It keeps you feeling full and satisfied all day, every day you are on it. And it enables you to lose more weight than you ever thought possible in the short time you follow it. It even comes in two versions: a seven-day plan, and a three-day blitz plan.

In the pages to come, you will learn what makes the Cabbage Soup Diet the quick weight-loss phenomenon it is, as well as how to follow it. But for now, let's take a look at what we know and don't know about its background.

The Sacred Heart Hospital Diet — Not

In the last year or so, the Cabbage Soup Diet has become the most talked-about — and one of the most popular — weight-loss plans of the nineties. Its fame among dieters grew without an army of promoters banging the drums for it; without medical endorsements; and until now, without even a book to explain what it's all about.

How did the excitement begin? Word of mouth. News of the diet spread from one enthusiastic dieter eager to share his or her weight-loss success to the next — face to face, by phone, by fax, and on the Internet. Soon, the Cabbage Soup Diet was being mentioned everywhere, both in the American and UK press, in magazines like *Cosmopolitan,* and on local and national TV. You've probably heard or read about this diet yourself — and perhaps the excitement you felt then even motivated you to buy this book!

Actually, there are several cabbage soup diets out there. Most of these versions are called simply the 'Cabbage Soup Diet'. But some have surfaced under such names as the 'Fat Burning Soup Diet', and the 'T-J Miracle Soup Diet'. It has also been called the 'Rochester Diet', the 'New Mayo Clinic Diet', and, most commonly, the 'Sacred Heart Hospital Diet'.

It's important to be clear right away that no Sacred Heart Hospital in America (and there are many — at least one in almost every area of the country) uses or recommends a diet based on cabbage soup to its patients, and neither does the Mayo Clinic. In fact, it is highly unlikely that the diet came from any big hospital or medical centre. Why do we say this?

Speed — The Critical Difference

The Cabbage Soup Diet gives you quick results. On the other hand, diets recommended by major medical institutions tend to work slowly, producing a one-to two-pound weight loss in a week or ten days. These diets are good, nutritionally sound plans. The slowness factor in all of them is built-in, partly to help dieters change their food habits over time. The thinking is that if we follow one of these snail's-pace diets long enough, we will gradually learn to make healthier food choices and incorporate the principles of good nutrition into our lives. When that happens, we may be able to keep our weight stable over the months and years.

Developing better eating habits is a worthwhile goal, one we should all strive for. But unfortunately, lack of early signs of success is also a major drawback of those same, snail's-pace weight-loss programs. Most of us go on diets wanting and hoping to see tangible results fairly quickly. But discouragement can set in when, after a week or ten days of dieting, the bathroom scale registers a loss of just a pound and a half or so. And for too many of us, discouragement leads to abandonment of the slow but steady and well-balanced diet. We may think, 'Oh, what's the use. At this rate, I'll never get rid of the pounds I want to lose.'

It's important to note that the sensible but slow-working diets endorsed by the nutrition establishment are models of good nutrition and excellent for the long haul, when a dieter wants and needs to lose forty, fifty, sixty pounds or more. But no matter who endorses it, a slow-working diet of any kind is among the least effective weight-loss plans if it turns you off at the beginning, when you are most eager to see signs of success, and when quick weight loss, momentum, and motivation matter most.

The Cabbage Soup Diet helps solve this classic diet problem — a problem in which impatience, frustration, and discouragement war against achieving substantial results. Use it for seven days and experience the gratification of quick weight loss. Then stop, wait two weeks, and go back to it again. Or, use it for seven days, actually see the results you've achieved as the diet propels you closer to your goal, then switch to a slower, long-term plan. In either case, the heightened confidence and motivation you get from a week of incredible diet success will help keep you on track and moving forward.

Mystery Diet? Maybe

But the question remains: if the Cabbage Soup Diet wasn't developed by a major medical institution, where did it come from? Unfortunately, we can only guess. Perhaps it was concocted by a lone doctor somewhere, a doctor who wanted to motivate certain patients to lose weight, and came up with a cabbage soup-based diet that would reward them with immediate results. Or, maybe it came from an innovative dieter who invented the cabbage soup plan while experimenting with foods he or she knew from experience could help take off pounds more quickly and easily than others.

In fact, the Cabbage Soup Diet, which includes some of the superfoods of the 90s (more about those in Chapter Two), may not be new at all. Some Internet users remember a cabbage soup diet from fifteen years ago. A dietitian at Sacred Heart Medical Center in Eugene, Oregon, said she thought it might be thirty years old or older!

That its origins are unclear, and that the diet was almost certainly not developed by a major health institution or obesity expert, is a problem for some people. We tend to place our faith in the importance and validity of a diet devised by experts. Not to mention the fact that diets associated with a major hospital, medical research organization, or well-known and well-placed obesity specialist have a certain cachet.

But not all experts are equal, they don't necessarily share the same views, and there are times when they question the merits of diets developed by other experts. Some of the new, high-protein, high-fat diets that have become best-selling books are perfect examples. They were developed by well-known weight-loss experts, yet some doctors and dietitians have been critical of these plans, which encourage us to eat all the meat, butter and dairy products we want.

So, while it can be reassuring to follow a diet planned by an expert, it is still important to keep in mind that there's more to a good weight-loss plan than a noted author. Mystery diet, or the creation of a world-famous expert, a good weight-loss plan must meet certain criteria.

If it's a diet you plan to use for weeks or months, was it developed in accordance with the rules of good nutrition? Can you imagine living with it for the duration? Does it really work?

When you use the Cabbage Soup Diet as it was meant to be used — for periods no longer than a week at a time followed by two weeks of normal eating — it is a safe and healthy food plan, packed with an abundance of all-important vegetables and fruits, and very low in fat. In fact, it is the best quick weight-loss diet around. During the seven days you're on it, it supplies all the nutrients you need to provide your body's needs, and to feel great, too! However, just like most ordinary, real-life eating, it does not supply all of them on every day. That's one of the reasons you are urged to stop the diet for two weeks after you've finished a seven-day cycle and shift into an improved version of your old way of eating for two weeks before repeating the diet.

The right food in the right amount is primary on any diet. But the Cabbage Soup Diet has other advantages, too: it keeps you feeling full and satisfied, so you can easily live with it, and on it, for the brief time you follow it. As for its effectiveness, it practically melts the pounds off, leaving you noticeably slimmer in just one week. At that point, your body and mind will be more prepared than they've ever been to help you keep on losing weight, or to maintain your weight loss by making sensible food choices.

Who Can Use the Cabbage Soup Diet?

The Cabbage Soup Diet is definitely not for children or adolescents. It may not be the best choice for people with certain medical conditions. But it's a superior quick weight-loss plan for just about everyone else: from first-time dieters, to the chronically disappointed who have tried everything without much success. From women and men who have been thin all their lives but suddenly notice an uncharacteristic, and minuscule, five- or ten-pound problem, to those who have been seriously overweight since childhood.

In a way, you might almost call the Cabbage Soup Diet a one-size-fits-all plan. It's that flexible. Want to lose the last few pounds you haven't been able to shake on an ordinary diet? Try the three-day blitz version (you'll find out more about it in Chapters Nine to Eleven). Want to take off the ten or fifteen pounds that piled on as a result of overenthusiastic holiday eating? A single seven-day cycle of the diet will probably do the trick. What about the twenty or thirty pounds that accumulated who knows when or how, and which make you look, and feel, years older than you are? The Cabbage Soup Diet gives you a choice: use it for seven days to get a head start on weight loss and achieve immediate, visible results, then finish up with a longer, slower diet, *or* use the diet for a week, eat a normal healthy diet for at least two weeks, then return to the diet periodically. If your weight problem is severe, use the Cabbage Soup Diet for seven days, to prove to yourself that yes, you can be a winner at weight loss, then ask a health professional to suggest a food plan you can follow until you achieve a healthy weight — or create your own slow but steady diet (you'll find out how in Chapter Sixteen).

Doctor's Permission First

Speak to your doctor before going on this or any other diet. Don't be surprised if he or she doesn't love this diet

— until you explain how you plan to use it: one week only, at intervals, or as a kickoff to another diet.

The Cabbage Soup Diet is strict, low in calories, and not meant to be a substitute for lifetime good nutrition. But the strictness and low calorie content are what make it such a miracle worker — and the one diet capable of solving problems that other diets simply do not address.

A Sneak Peek at the Prototype Diet

The several versions of the Cabbage Soup Diet that have come to light in recent months probably evolved as individual dieters put their own spin on the basic plan. This version, which came from the Internet, may be the prototype. Take a look at it, note the general principles, but don't use it. There's a new and improved version coming up in the next chapter.

Cabbage Soup Diet Prototype

You may have as much as you want of the mainstay of this diet — cabbage soup — and you can have it as often as you want it throughout the diet.

★ Note ★

Fruits and vegetables that are very low in calories are called 'free' on the Cabbage Soup Diet. On certain days of the diet you are allowed to have as many of these free fruits or vegetables as you want.

Day 1

Unlimited cabbage soup
Unlimited free fruits
Unsweetened tea or coffee; cranberry juice; water

Day 2
Unlimited cabbage soup
Unlimited free vegetables
1 large baked potato with butter
Unsweetened tea or coffee; cranberry juice; water

Day 3
Unlimited cabbage soup
Unlimited free fruit
Unlimited free vegetables
Unsweetened tea or coffee; cranberry juice; water

Day 4
Unlimited cabbage soup
3 to 6 bananas
8 glasses skimmed milk
Unsweetened tea or coffee; cranberry juice; water

Day 5
Unlimited cabbage soup
10 to 20 ounces of beef or skinless chicken
1 28-ounce can of tomatoes or up to 6 fresh tomatoes
Unsweetened tea or coffee; cranberry juice; water

Day 6
Unlimited cabbage soup
Unlimited beef
Unlimited vegetables, including tomatoes
Unsweetened tea or coffee; cranberry juice; water

Day 7
Unlimited cabbage soup
Unlimited brown rice

Unlimited free vegetables
Unsweetened tea or coffee; cranberry juice; water

Remember, do not use the prototype diet in this chapter. It was included here for reference, to give you an idea of what the Cabbage Soup Diet is all about, and so you'll be able to compare it to the New Cabbage Soup Diet coming up in Chapter Three. The differences between the two may seem slight, yet they are significant. But rest assured, the new version is right in line with the basic diet that has made a coast-to-coast impact on thousands of people who have used it successfully to achieve their personal diet goals.

'Magic' Ingredients

As we've seen, there are no strange or exotic foods on the Cabbage Soup Diet, only a wholesome and varied selection of many of the ordinary foods you've been eating all along. There are a few unusual combinations, and some unexpected changes in content on days five and six. But 'magic'? Hardly. The origins of the diet may be a mystery, but there's no mystery about the healthy foods you'll be enjoying when you start your first cycle of cabbage soup diet eating. There's no monumental weight-loss breakthrough here, either. Nothing but good foods that nutrition experts and ordinary dieters have known about for years. In the next chapter, we're going to take an even closer look at the food, as well as at the reasons why this diet has become such an extraordinary success.

a closer look at the cabbage soup diet

The original Cabbage Soup Diet and the New Cabbage Soup Diet, revealed in Chapter Three, have a lot of good things in common: they're equally effective at getting rid of pounds in a hurry. They're easy to follow and keep you feeling full and satisfied from start to finish. They're high-motivation diets that give you the impetus you need to face down challenges and keep going until you achieve your goal. Many of the foods that make both of the cabbage soup diets — the old, prototype version and the New Cabbage Soup Diet — such powerful, quick weight-loss tools are the same. And, of course, cabbage soup is the basis of each. For a better idea of why cabbage soup is the key to success on these diets, let's take an ingredient-by-ingredient look at what's in it.

Diet Soup and Health Soup

There is nothing miraculous about a bowl of this cabbage soup; it is a wonderfully nutritious and good-tasting mix of vegetables — and all the quick weight-loss benefits they provide.

Cabbage is the 'star' of this soup. It's quick-cooking, low-cost, and available in practically every supermarket throughout the year. And it's packed with nutrients that make it a great nutritional bargain, particularly the humble, garden-variety kind you'll use to make the soup.

Cabbage is high in fibre, vitamin C, and potassium. Its robust, earthy flavour is quickly suffused into the stock or broth it is cooked in. Cabbage is a member of the cruciferous family of vegetables (a few of the other crucifers are cauliflower, broccoli, and brussels sprouts). Various studies indicate that women and men who consume large amounts of these vegetables are less likely to develop certain types of cancer. (Cabbage and other cruciferous vegetables, however, do not *cure* cancer.) Like most vegetables, cabbage is virtually fat free. And it's so low in calories — a cup of raw shredded cabbage has only about seventeen — you could eat it by the pound and still lose weight. But, of course, you won't need to eat it by the pound on the Cabbage Soup Diet — only as much as you want.

The other veggies in the soup — carrots, red peppers, onions, spring onions, and celery — are just as good for you.

Carrots, for example, also provide fibre, and are a rich source of vitamin A and its precursor, cancer-preventive beta-carotene. In fact, carrots are one of the very best ways to get beta-carotene into your diet; a one-half cup serving of cooked carrots provides more beta-carotene than you get in a similar portion of almost any other vegetable! At about thirty calories per medium carrot, this vegetable, too, gives you an abundance of important nutrients at a very low cost in calories.

Green and red peppers are both high in vitamin C, good sources of vitamin A and potassium, and very low in calories; one cup of cubed green or red pepper has about twenty-five calories.

Onions deliver potassium, some protein, and fibre, but their main contribution to the soup is delectable flavor and aroma. A cup of cooked onion sliced into bite-size pieces has about sixty calories. Spring onions, also part of the basic soup recipe, are sometimes called scallions. They have a fair amount of potassium and fibre as well as traces of protein. Like bulb-shaped onions, their chief role in the soup is to enhance the flavour of other ingredients, and this they do at a caloric cost of only about thirty-five calories a cup.

Tomatoes have good amounts of vitamins A, C, and potassium, and deliver some niacin (a component of the B-vitamin complex). Their flavour adds richness and complexity to soups and broths. Being mostly water, tomatoes are very low in calories; a whole pound delivers only about ninety-five. Because tomatoes are compacted and condensed during the canning process, a cup of stewed tomatoes has about ninety calories.

Celery, the final vegetable ingredient in the soup, contributes subtle flavour, fibre, and potassium to the mix. Like tomatoes, celery is mostly water, which accounts for its very low calorie content; one-half cup of diced celery contains about twenty calories.

The basic recipe also calls for water, plus onion soup mix, bouillon cubes, and other ingredients that add flavour to the soup.

As you will see when you take a look at the new and improved version of the soup, in Chapter Three, it contains all the healthy veggies listed above, along with another ingredient that makes it even more nutritious. The new version omits the high-sodium flavouring ingredients, without any loss of taste appeal, which makes it a better food for those who must watch their salt intake. Plus, you'll find some terrific low-cal ideas for quickly and simply varying the basic soup flavour in Chapter Six.

Cabbage Soup and the Superfoods for 2000

Nutritious, and low in fat and calories, the cabbage soup that forms the basis of the new and old versions of the Cabbage Soup Diet also contains good amounts of certain nutrients that the International Food Information Council (IFIC) describes as containing 'significant levels of biologically active components that impart health benefits beyond basic nutrition when consumed in typical or optimal serving sizes.' Some experts call foods containing these biologically active substances 'functional foods', but they're also known informally as 'superfoods'. These food components aren't new; they've always been present in many of the ordinary fruits, vegetables, grains, and other foods that have been part of the human diet for thousands of years.

But it wasn't until recently that we began to recognize their beneficial effects.

Antioxidants

Some of the vegetables included in the basic cabbage soup recipe fall into the superfood category because they contain antioxidants that help defend us against a range of diseases — and are even believed to slow the ageing process! Scientists have known about antioxidants for decades, but their role in human nutrition was not well understood until a few years ago.

How do antioxidants work? As the body uses oxygen to create energy, cells throughout the body produce by-products called 'free radicals'. These by-products can cause physical damage to the cells and interfere with the DNA that controls their growth. Large numbers of damaged cells, in turn, make the body more vulnerable to many diseases including cancer, heart disease, stroke, cataracts, and can result in early signs of ageing. Free-radical formation is natural and inevitable, but some of the damage it causes can be prevented by antioxidants, which surround and neutralize them before they have a chance to wreak havoc. In other words, consuming foods that contain ample amounts of antioxidants helps keep cells intact and healthier, thereby reducing the risk for many diseases, and slowing the degeneration that takes place in the body over the years.

Among the big-gun antioxidants are vitamin C, beta-carotene (a precursor to vitamin A), and vitamin E. Vitamin C and beta-carotene, as we've seen, are plentiful in the basic cabbage soup vegetables and in many of the 'free' vegetables and fruits you'll be enjoying on this diet.

Phytochemicals

'Phyto' (pronounced fye-toe, with the accent on the 'fye') refers to plants, and the word 'phytochemical' refers to compounds that give a plant its distinctive colour, scent, and flavour. Antioxidants are often classed as phytochemicals (some of the pigments that give colour to fruits and vegetables are antioxidants), but not all phytochemicals are antioxidants. Ten years ago, most nutrition scientists were unaware of the existence of many of these compounds, let alone the important role they play in human nutrition. Now phytochemicals are the subject of some of today's hottest nutrition news because of the unexpected benefits they provide to us through the food we eat.

All fruits and vegetables are plants or parts of plants, and all plants produce phytochemicals, many of which seem to work in combination with others. Scientists continue to discover more phytochemicals as research into this fascinating area moves forward, so we still don't know how many different phytochemicals there are. But we do have a pretty good idea of what the known ones contribute to our well-being. A complete list would take up pages in this book, so let's focus on a handful of known phytochemicals that are abundant in the foods you'll be eating on the Cabbage Soup Diet.

1. Indoles form an important group of phytochemicals and are present in cabbage.

Indoles appear to make it easier for the body to get rid of toxins through excretion. Some researchers suspect that it may be the indoles in cabbage that give it — as well as its relatives, broccoli, brussels sprouts, and kale — its cancer preventive properties.

2. Allium. Onions and members of the onion family, including chives and garlic, contain allium, which may lower cholesterol levels and neutralize some cancer-causing chemicals in the body.

3. Carotenoids (a group that includes beta-carotene) are abundant in carrots and may protect body cells from various toxins.

4. Lycopene, a compound that gives many red vegetables — such as tomatoes — their brilliant colour may protect against cancer of the stomach, bladder, and colon. A Harvard study found that men who ate several servings a week of tomatoes and tomato-based products lowered their risk for prostate cancer by half. Red peppers, which you can substitute for green in the cabbage soup recipe are good sources of lycopene.

5. Coumarin, also found in tomatoes, may help prevent blood clots in the body.

The vitamins, minerals, antioxidants, and phytochemicals present in the cabbage soup and other elements of the diet are musts for good health. But they're not the only valuable compounds you get when you eat according to the Cabbage Soup Diet. Fibre deserves a few brief paragraphs of its own.

The Fibre Factor

Fibre has no nutrititive value. Unlike vitamins, it's not essential to human life and growth. Yet it is very important to good nutrition, and is a major element of both the old and the new versions of the Cabbage Soup Diet. Fibre, you see, appears to increase the amount of fat excreted by the body, and this in turn may accelerate the weight-loss process. Fibre certainly fills you up at little or no cost in calories, as scientific research has borne out. In one study, volunteers who were served a diet high in fibre consumed significantly fewer calories than they normally did, even though they were instructed to eat as much as they wanted.

What is it about fibre that makes it so useful in weight control? Fibre is absorbent. Because it soaks up water and begins to swell as it passes through the upper part of the digestive tract, fibre promotes long-lasting feelings of fullness.

Fibre itself is non-nutritive and delivers no calories, so it fills you up without adding to your calorie intake for the day. (Of course, fibre-rich foods are not necessarily low in calories — especially if you doctor them up with fatty add-ons like butter or oil).

Fibre, because it is so filling, also tends to reduce your calorie intake by 'displacing' other, higher calorie foods. After a high-fibre first course you just won't be as eager for those other foods.

Fibre also helps keep blood sugar levels steadier by slowing the digestion of carbohydrates. Low blood sugar can make you feel fatigued or irritable, and when blood sugar levels swing down low enough, your body may respond by calling out for more food.

As you probably know already, there are many other advantages to be gained by consuming good amounts of fibre. There is evidence, for example, that certain types of fibre reduce the amount of fat and cholesterol in the bloodstream; this in turn seems to decrease the risk of heart disease. Fibre also lowers colon cancer risk and makes diverticulosis (a disease in which the intestinal wall develops 'pockets') and appendicitis less likely. Fibre research is ongoing, and this important substance in our food may turn out to have even more benefits than the important ones we already know about.

There are two kinds of fibre, soluble and insoluble. The soluble kind lowers blood cholesterol and keeps blood sugar levels on an even keel. Insoluble fibre reduces the risk of colon cancer, diverticulosis, and appendicitis. The range of vegetables and fruits that make up the bulk of the cabbage soup diets, old and new, deliver both types of fibre in abundance.

Calories Do Count

But from a dieter's point of view, what's most important about the original Cabbage Soup Diet and the new one, revealed in Chapter Three, is that they are low in calories. In fact, many of the vegetables you read about earlier in this chapter are so low in calories that you can eat huge amounts of them without taking in the minimum number of calories your body needs each day. Some of those vegetables actually provide fewer calories than your body uses in chewing, swallowing, and digesting them. The negative value of these calories helps explain why dieters can fill up on the soup four or five times a day if they want to — and still experience dramatic weight loss in just a few days.

The idea of denying your body the calories it needs may make you a little uncomfortable. But if you're healthy, and your weight problem is not complicated by genetic factors, it's the only way to lose weight, other than to boost your activity levels way above what's normal for you. (Getting more exercise is important, of course, and you'll find out how to incorporate moderate exercise into your life later on in this book.) Low-calorie and negative-calorie eating are essential to the weight-loss process, which occurs when your body is forced to turn to its own fat deposits for fuel. To repeat: the pounds won't budge as long as you take in more calories than your body needs for fuel.

The very low-calorie and negative-calorie aspects of the Cabbage Soup Diet make it a distant relative of some of the low-calorie diets you might remember from the past. These diets typically called for eating large amounts of a very limited selection of low-calorie foods — like grapefruit, for example, or rice, or salad greens — and they usually stressed consuming no more than a certain number of calories each day. Now we hardly ever hear about calorie counting, or calorie cutting. The emphasis has shifted to limiting dietary fat.

The Fetish for Low Fat

The New Cabbage Soup Diet and the old are both very low in calories and very low in fat, which is the most concentrated source of calories. But, except for plain, no-fat yoghurt and fat-reduced salad dressing in the case of the New Cabbage Soup Diet, neither cabbage soup diet instructs you to use low-fat versions of ordinary foods, such as low-fat cookies or cakes, low-fat snack foods, or low-fat frozen deserts.

Overreliance on fat-reduced foods may be a cause of what some experts have called 'the obesity epidemic' of recent years. Those experts are referring to the unexpected increase in the percentage of overweight people in the 1980s and 1990s as documented by a long-term study conducted in the USA by the federal Centers for Disease Control and Prevention. According to that study, about 20 percent of the population in the 1960s and 1970s were obese. However, by the early 1990s, more than 30 percent of Americans were obese. That translates into about 58 million people who today weigh at least 20 percent more than their ideal body weight. The percentage increase seemed to have little or nothing to do with the ageing of the population because it was evident in all age groups. In other words, today's forty-year-olds on average weigh more than forty-year-olds did in 1970. It's the same with children, young adults, and older people.

What happened during that time? For one thing, a barrage of reports and studies were released linking dietary fat to heart disease, various types of cancer, diabetes, and other conditions — including, of course, obesity. Soon, a spate of books and magazine articles emphasizing dietary fat as the primary and even the sole factor in being overweight were published. At the same time food technologists were developing methods of producing a wide range of products using less fat, and these items began to show up in supermarkets with words like 'lower fat', 'reduced fat', or 'fat-free' on their labels. Millions of people, newly aware of the importance of consuming less fat, began to use these foods.

But for large numbers of them, the words 'low fat' on a label gave them permission to 'go ahead, eat all you want.' And they did. Their logic went something like this: fat is the culprit. Fat makes you more vulnerable to killer diseases. And fat makes you fat. Ergo, food from which most of the fat has been removed is okay. It won't put you at risk for serious disease, and it won't make you fat. People who used to watch their calories began to watch their fat intake instead. And some began eating large amounts of high-sugar or high-starch foods that were low in fat, as well as the entire range of reduced-fat foods — from reduced-fat cookies, cakes, and snacks, to low-fat ham and other cold cuts, to low-fat cheese and other dairy products.

But low fat isn't the same as low calorie. And in fact, many reduced-fat foods, like lower fat ice cream, are laden with calories. When Americans started filling up on low fat but calorific foods, the gross national weight skyrocketed. The scenario is only one of several put forward by experts to explain why millions of people weigh more in the 1990s than their counterparts did in the 1970s, but it's an important one.

Of course, you should cut down on fat wherever possible. You'll be less vulnerable to certain diseases, if you do. You'll feel better and you'll probably look better. Simply reducing your fat intake might even produce considerable weight loss over time, especially if you have been in the habit of consuming large amounts of fatty meats, fatty sauces and spreads, fried foods, and fatty desserts when you started. Low-fat and no-fat foods, because they help you to reduce the fat in your diet, have a useful and important role to play in good nutrition today. But calories count, too, and for those of us who want to lose weight, it's important not to make the mistake of replacing fatty foods with greater amounts of reduced-fat items.

Whoever developed the Cabbage Soup Diet was keenly aware of the importance of low-calorie, as well as low-fat eating for quick weight loss, because she or he kept the calorie and fat content as low as they can be without sacrificing many vital nutrients. Cutting calories while you cut the fat may be an old-fashioned idea, but it is regaining popularity as more and more people today begin to recognize that simply reducing dietary fat — though extremely important to good health — is not the only change we need to make to get rid of excess pounds.

As you can see from this up-close look at what makes the Cabbage Soup Diet work, the food you'll be eating when you start the diet is much more than just good diet food. It's good food, good for anyone, anytime. In the next chapter you'll see why the New Cabbage Soup Diet is even better than the old one.

the new and improved cabbage soup diet revealed

Why on earth change the Cabbage Soup Diet? It's already one of the most popular, most written-about, most successful quick weight-loss programs in the country. It already has dieters from coast to coast raving about the dramatic results they've experienced in seven days or less. It's already the most highly effective and versatile approach to a variety of diet situations:

• You can go on the three-day version anytime you need to slim down enough to fit into a favourite dress or suit for an important event.
• You can follow the seven-day version for a visible, ten-pound loss that makes a big difference in the way you look and feel.
• You can use the diet as a quick-start, high-motivation kickoff to a slower, longer-term weight-loss programme that will leave you not only slimmer, but

healthier and less vulnerable to serious diseases.

• And you can use it periodically, as long as you allow at least two weeks between each diet cycle.

So why change the diet? For two simple reasons. To make sure you get even better, quicker results. And to make it more nutritious.

Even though the original, unmodified Cabbage Soup Diet gives you the solution to just about any diet problem, there's room for improvement. The New Cabbage Soup Diet is equally good for addressing those problems. But the changes in the plan make it easier to follow and better for you.

What's Wrong With the Old Cabbage Soup Diet?

The old Cabbage Soup Diet provides you with an abundance of good, healthy food. But it falls short when it comes to certain food groups. If you review the prototype Cabbage Soup Diet in Chapter One, you'll see that some important food groups are excluded or underused and one food is overused. The old version falls short in the following areas:

Protein
The need for protein, particularly animal protein, was overemphasized until fairly recently. Nevertheless, every organ of your body needs and uses protein, which is essential to growth and tissue repair and is important to a well-functioning immune system. The old Cabbage Soup Diet falls short, except for Days 5 and 6, when you can fill up on beef or chicken.

Grains

There are no grains on the old Cabbage Soup Diet other than the brown rice on Day 7. Grains are important sources of B vitamins and provide some iron.

Calcium

The old version of the diet is too low in calcium except for Day 4, when you are instructed to drink eight glasses of skimmed milk. Calcium, of course, is essential for strong bones and teeth and can help prevent bone loss in adults. Osteoporosis, a condition in which bones become porous and fragile, is a major health problem in many older people. Adequate calcium throughout life can help reduce the risk for this disease in later years.

Beef

The old Cabbage Soup Diet allows large amounts of beef on days 5 and 6. Though there's a place for red meat, in moderation, on any sensible, long-term food plan, whether you are dieting or not, beef contains saturated fats and has too many calories for optimal quick weight loss.

The Boredom Factor

The old Cabbage Soup Diet is long on plain, good-tasting food, but short on variety. It provided nothing in the way of flavour and texture variations, and the result is a certain sameness from meal to meal and day to day. Variety is important. It's a source of gratification and satisfaction in itself. Further, interesting food, because it helps us feel less deprived, can help us remain committed to the weight-loss process.

The New Cabbage Soup Diet — Much Better

All the above issues have been addressed in turning the Cabbage Soup Diet into the New Cabbage Soup Diet — which offers better nutrition, more variety, and better results.

Protein Boost

Animal protein

As you probably remember from school or college nutrition courses, proteins are made up of twenty-two amino acids, nine of which are not produced within the human body. We can get complete protein — the kind that includes all twenty-two amino acids — from many foods of animal origin, including meat and fish, eggs, milk and other dairy products, as well as from some soybean-based foods.

The protein content of the New Cabbage Soup Diet gets a boost with the inclusion of your choice of plain, no-fat yoghurt or skimmed milk, both foods of animal origin. On the new version of the diet, you'll be having eight ounces of either per day.

★ Note ★

Switching between skimmed milk and plain, no-fat yogurt in the course of a single day is not allowed. You must decide at the beginning of each day whether you want it to be a milk day or a yoghurt day.

Plant protein

Plant foods also supply protein. But with the exception of certain foods made with soybeans, no single plant — be it a grain, a vegetable, or a fruit — supplies all nine of the essential amino acids. For that reason, protein from plants is sometimes referred to as 'incomplete'.

However, when your diet includes a variety of plant foods, the chances are good that you will be getting good amounts of complete protein. That's because different plant foods supply different combinations of amino acids — and if you consume a variety of vegetables and other foods of plant origin — as you will on the Cabbage Soup Diet — the various amino acids combine to produce complete proteins.

Here's where one of the older dictates of good nutrition comes in for some debunking: nutrition scientists used to believe that the only way to make sure the body got sufficient complete protein from plant foods was to eat a grain product (such as bread or pasta or rice), with beans, peas, or lentils at the same meal. Now they recognize that this kind of meal-planning isn't necessary and that these two types of plant foods do not need to be eaten at the same meal for complete protein to result. Eating a variety of plant foods over the course of a day or so can be enough.

To give you a wider variety of plant foods from which your body can pick and choose to make complete proteins, brown rice has been added to each day of the New Cabbage Soup Diet. You'll be having it as a soup ingredient in amounts that provide you with approximately one-quarter cup of rice each day.

Going with the Grains

The same brown rice that is used to boost the protein content of the soup, also makes up for some of the diet's grain deficiency. Brown rice is specified because it provides more in the way of vitamins and other nutrients than white rice.

To understand the difference, first imagine a grain of rice in its natural state. It's covered with a tough husk. Under that, there's a layer of bran. The bran in turn surrounds the endosperm. In white rice, the husk and bran are removed, leaving only the endosperm and germ. Brown rice, however, retains most of the bran. Bran is what gives brown rice its darker colour, nuttier flavour, and chewier texture. Bran also contributes more and better nutrients, including larger amounts of better-quality plant protein, more fibre, more B complex vitamins, some vitamin E (an antioxidant), which is not present in white rice, and good amounts of potassium. The downside is that brown rice takes longer to cook than the white kind. (It's just as easy to cook as white rice, however.) A fifteen-minute increase in cooking time is a pretty small price to pay for the increase in important food elements you get in return.

Calcium Upgrade

Rice does double-duty on the New Cabbage Soup Diet by contributing vegetable protein and supplying good amounts of the important nutrients found in grains, as well. The skimmed milk or yoghurt you will be eating every day on the new version of the diet is also a two-for-one addition. Both provide more complete protein, as we've already seen, and more calcium.

Consuming milk and milk products — like yoghurt — is the best-known and surest way to get more calcium into your body, which is why the New Cabbage Soup Diet includes one cup of skimmed milk or plain, no-fat yoghurt daily. (Removing the fat from these foods does not reduce their calcium content. Fat-free milk and yoghurt deliver as much calcium as you'd get from equal amounts of whole milk or regular yoghurt.)

To be sure, one cup of either of these two foods does not supply the body's total daily requirement for this important mineral. Many experts recommend at least two cups of milk or yoghurt daily, plus several servings of other calcium-rich foods as a way of insuring adequate amounts of calcium. You can augment the calcium you get from milk or yoghurt by choosing calcium-rich vegetables on days when free vegetables are on the diet menu. Some of the best vegetable sources of calcium are listed here for your convenience:

Good Vegetable Sources of Calcium

Leafy green vegetables: romaine lettuce, spinach, escarole, collard greens, kale, watercress, chicory, and parsley. Nonleafy vegetables: broccoli, cauliflower, asparagus.

Have at least one of these vegetables on days when free vegetables are part of the diet.

Where's the Beef?

On Day 5 of the original Cabbage Soup Diet you may have ten to twenty ounces of beef, and on Day 6 you may have as much beef as you like. That's too much beef. All cuts of beef, including hamburger, contain fat. Even if the beef is lean to begin with and you trim away as much visible fat as you can, it's still impossible to avoid fat entirely when you consume beef. As if that's not a good enough reason to make the change from beef to something else on Day 5, consider the fact that beef fat is saturated fat, laden with cholesterol.

Better choices, that are lower in fat and calories, are grilled or roasted chicken and grilled fish. Do these replacements for beef really make a big difference? Yes, perhaps an even bigger difference than you thought.

There are about 197 calories in very lean grilled ground beef and about 242 calories in four ounces of grilled lean T-bone steak. But there are only 159 calories in four ounces of grilled halibut, and 149 calories in grilled snapper. As for chicken, one breast, without the skin, has about 141 calories; a chicken thigh without skin has 108 calories, and one drumstick without skin has 76 calories.

To keep calories, fat, and cholesterol in the diet as low as possible, and yet provide good amounts of animal protein, the New Cabbage Soup Diet calls for unlimited grilled or roasted fish or chicken on Days 5 and 6.

★ Note ★

Feel free to alternate between fish or chicken on both days.

More Flavouring

No flavouring ingredients were mentioned in the old Cabbage Soup Diet, not even salt and pepper. Since we don't know who created the diet, it's impossible to ask if there was a reason for this omission, or whether it was just an oversight. What we do know, however, is that there are dozens of no-fat, no-cal, and low-cal ways to add more zing to the diet. Because taste appeal is important even on a quick weight-loss plan such as this one, a range of seasonings and other flavour ingredients has been added. You can perk up your food with your choice of fresh or dried herbs, spices, hot sauces, soy sauce, vinegars, ketchup, or lemon juice — in short, just about any no- or low-cal ingredient you can think of. You can also use one tablespoon per day of no- or low-fat prepared salad dressings.

Oils, and oily salad dressings, rich sauces, butter, margarine, and other high-fat or high-calorie condiments are taboo, of course.

In Chapter Six you will find suggestions and ideas for pumping up the flavour of all the foods on the New Cabbage Soup Diet, including the soup.

Other New Cabbage Soup Diet Changes in Brief

The major change is on Day 7. If you look at the old Cabbage Soup Diet plan in Chapter One, you'll see that on Day 7 you are directed to eat as much cabbage soup as you want, and to have unlimited amounts of brown rice, unlimited amounts of free vegetables, and as much unsweetened fruit juice as you care to drink. The cabbage soup, of course, is part of every day on the diet but it's not clear why the person who originated the diet decided that you and others should fill up on brown rice that day, or what purpose is served by drinking unlimited fruit juice. The big switch to brown rice seems arbitrary, in fact.

As you know, many, many dieters are thrilled with the number of pounds they lost on the diet, and there are times when it's best not to quarrel with success. However, this isn't one of them. Since brown rice is a part of the new cabbage soup recipe, and you will be receiving some of its nutritional advantages every day on the New Cabbage Soup Diet, the unlimited brown rice allowed on Day 7 of the old diet has been eliminated.

As for all that unsweetened fruit juice, it does deliver most of the nutrients you'd get in fruit. But it's not as filling and satisfying as whole fruit, and provides considerably less fibre. The question is, why unlimited fruit juice on Day 7, instead of unlimited fruit? Though the juice may provide a nice change of pace for people who prefer it to whole fresh fruit, there is no logical answer to the question. The unlimited fruit juice on Day 7 has been removed for that reason.

With these changes, Day 7 of the New Cabbage Soup Diet, now offers unlimited soup, unlimited vegetables and unlimited fruit. It is, in fact, identical to Day 4, and a much more satisfying and logical way to end the week.

No Cranberry Juice

The reason for excluding cranberry juice as a drink option in the new version of the diet is simple. There are 144 calories in a cup of cranberry juice, and though it tastes good and contributes more vitamin C to the diet, the cost in calories isn't worth it.

No Butter

Many dieters are surprised to see butter included as an accompaniment to baked potato on Day 3 of the old Cabbage Soup Diet. A tablespoon of butter delivers 102 calories and 31 milligrams of cholesterol. Even if you used just a pat of butter (one teaspoon) you'd be getting 36 calories and 11 milligrams of cholesterol. You don't need it.

No Onion Soup Mix or Bouillon Cubes for the Soup

These items are included in the old cabbage soup

ingredient list to give the soup heartier flavour. In fact, their main contribution to the soup is salt and other seasonings such as monosodium glutamate (which is used liberally in many soup mixes and bouillon cubes or powders), as well as a few calories. With the exception of the salt, none of the onion soup mix ingredients is essential to your enjoyment of the soup. It's the same with the bouillon cubes.

It's better to add your own seasonings to the soup. That way, you can adjust the salt exactly to your taste, rather than consume it in the large amounts you get when you add soup mix or bouillon cubes. You can also vary other flavourings any way you want to. In Chapter Six you will find several suggestions for adding spices, sauces, and other ingredients that add great flavour to the soup.

Artificial Sweetener for Tea or Coffee

The old Cabbage Soup Diet specified unsweetened tea or coffee. It's not hard to understand why the old version prohibits sugar, at 23 calories per packet, but there's no reason in the world why you shouldn't use artificial sweetener at 4 calories per packet. If you want to sweeten your favourite hot beverage with an artificial sweetener, go ahead.

Old vs. New Cabbage Soup Diets — No Contest!

Now that you know how the New Cabbage Soup Diet is different from the old version this day-by-day overview of each will put the changes into perspective.

Here's the original Cabbage Soup Diet:

Day 1
Cabbage Soup, unlimited amounts
Free fruits, unlimited amounts
Unsweetened tea or coffee; cranberry juice; water

Day 2
Cabbage Soup
Free vegetables, unlimited amounts
1 large baked potato with butter
Unsweetened tea or coffee; cranberry juice; water

Day 3
Cabbage Soup
Free fruits and vegetables, unlimited amounts
Unsweetened tea or coffee; cranberry juice; water

Day 4
Cabbage Soup
3 to 6 bananas
8 glasses of skimmed milk
Unsweetened tea or coffee; cranberry juice; water

Day 5
10 to 20 ounces of beef or skinless chicken
1 28-ounce can of tomatoes or as many as 6 fresh
tomatoes
Unsweetened tea or coffee; cranberry juice; water

Day 6
Cabbage Soup
Unlimited free vegetables, including tomatoes

Beef, as much as you want
Unsweetened tea or coffee; cranberry juice; water

Day 7
Cabbage Soup
Unlimited brown rice
Unlimited free vegetables
Unlimited fruit juice (including cranberry juice)
Unsweetened tea or coffee; water

Now here's how the New Cabbage Soup Diet stacks up:

Day 1
Cabbage soup
Unlimited free fruits
1 8-ounce serving of skimmed milk, or plain, low-fat yoghurt
Tea or coffee, plain, or with artificial sweetener
1 tablespoon low- or no-fat salad dressing
Your choice of low-cal or no-cal herbs, spices, and other flavouring ingredients

Day 2
Cabbage Soup
Unlimited free vegetables
1 8-ounce serving of skimmed milk, or plain, low-fat yoghurt
1 large baked potato
Tea or coffee, plain, or with artificial sweetener
1 tablespoon low- or no-fat salad dressing
Your choice of low-cal or no-cal herbs, spices, and other flavouring ingredients

Day 3

Cabbage Soup
Unlimited free vegetables
Unlimited free fruits
1 8-ounce serving of skimmed milk, or plain, low-fat yoghurt
Tea or coffee, plain, or with artificial sweetener
1 tablespoon low- or no-fat salad dressing
Your choice of low-cal or no-cal herbs, spices, and other flavouring ingredients

Day 4

Cabbage Soup
3 to 6 bananas
8 8-ounce glasses skimmed milk, or 1 8-ounce serving plain, low-fat yoghurt and 7 8-ounce glasses skimmed milk

Day 5

Cabbage Soup
Unlimited grilled fish
Unlimited grilled chicken
1 28-ounce can tomatoes, or up to 6 fresh tomatoes
1 8-ounce serving skimmed milk, or plain, low-fat yoghurt
Tea or coffee, plain, or with artificial sweetener
1 tablespoon low- or no-fat salad dressing
Your choice of low-cal or no-cal herbs, spices, and other flavouring ingredients

Day 6

Cabbage soup
Unlimited grilled fish

Unlimited grilled chicken
Unlimited free vegetables, including tomatoes
1 8-ounce serving skimmed-milk, or plain, low-fat yoghurt
Tea or coffee, plain, or with artificial sweetener
1 tablespoon low- or no-fat salad dressing
Your choice of low-cal or no-cal herbs, spices, and other flavouring ingredients

Day 7
Unlimited free vegetables
Unlimited free fruits
1 8-ounce serving of skimmed milk, or plain, low-fat yoghurt
Tea or coffee, plain, or with artificial sweetener
1 tablespoon low- or no-fat salad dressing
Your choice of low-cal or no-cal herbs, spices, and other flavouring ingredients

The New and Improved Cabbage Soup Diet
Rice in the soup, more skimmed milk or yoghurt, artificial sweetener, one tablespoon of low- or no-fat salad dressing, your choice of low-cal seasonings, no beef, no butter, and no cranberry juice — those are the simple changes that make the New and Improved Cabbage Soup Diet tastier, healthier, and even better for getting rid of pounds in a hurry than the original version.

In the next chapter you'll find out more about the nutritious food you'll be eating when you start your first cycle of the New Cabbage Soup Diet — including the best free fruits and vegetables, and how to shop for them and which fish and chicken varieties are lowest in fat. Plus, of course, how to make the great-tasting cabbage soup that gives the diet its name.

how to make the soup
plus
food tips for this phenomenal diet

You know the ingredients and the structure of the New Cabbage Soup Diet. You're almost ready for your first week of the diet, and the speedy results you'll get with it. But this amazing diet, like every other diet you've ever tried or heard about, requires some advance planning. You have to make the soup. You have to shop ahead for the fresh, frozen, or canned vegetables and fruits you'll be enjoying on this amazing diet. You have to select low-fat chicken and/or fish for Days 5 and 6. In short, you have to prepare.

First, the Soup
You don't need to be a good cook to make the soup. You don't need to know how to cook at all. All you need to do is read and follow these very simple directions.

★ Important ★

The recipe below makes about 12 pints of soup. If you do not own a 12-pint pot you can easily halve the recipe by using only half of each ingredient.

You'll need almost two hours in all to make the soup. It takes approximately twenty minutes to chop the vegetables; about a half hour for the soup to come to a boil; and about an hour of simmering to soften the vegetables and bring out their flavours.

Cabbage Soup

To make 12 pints of soup, you'll need:

1 head cabbage
6 carrots
6 medium onions
6 spring onions
2 green or red peppers
3 whole tomatoes, or 1 28-ounce can of tomatoes
5 stalks celery
½ cup uncooked brown rice.

Salt and pepper to taste. (For ideas on how to vary the flavour with low- or no-cal herbs, spices, and other flavouring ingredients, see Chapter Eight.)

Cut the vegetables into bite-size pieces. If you are using whole canned tomatoes, cut these into pieces, too. Place vegetables in a large, 12-pint pot, and add enough cold water to cover.

Boil for ten minutes, uncovered, then cover the pot and simmer over low heat until all the vegetables are soft. This will take about one hour. (Some people like to bring out even more intense vegetable flavour by simmering the soup for longer periods.)

While the soup is simmering, cook ½ cup of brown rice according to package directions. Add cooked rice to the soup when the soup is almost finished. Add salt and pepper to taste when the soup is fully cooked.

That's it! Now you have 12 pints of healthy, great-tasting cabbage soup. Freeze half of it in a large plastic container. Store the rest in the refrigerator so it will be ready whenever you want it.

Have It Hot!

Cabbage soup is the mainstay of the New Cabbage Soup Diet. You will be enjoying the soup every day for lunch and dinner. To keep you feeling full and satisfied throughout the diet, you may also have the soup in any amount, at any time of day or night, on any day of the diet. Hot foods are much more satisfying than lukewarm or cold, so be sure to heat the soup on top of the stove or in the microwave before you eat it.

Shopping Spree-Free Vegetables and Fruits

It's extremely important to follow the New Cabbage Soup Diet to the letter. In order to do that, you will need to shop ahead so that you'll have enough of the right foods on hand when you need them. You'll need to know which vegetables and fruits qualify as 'free' varieties — the ones you can have in unlimited quantities anytime you want them. And of those, you'll need to know how to select the ones that deliver the best nutrition and the most delicious and satisfying flavour.

The day before you start the New Cabbage Soup

Diet is the day to shop for much of what you'll need. If you're planning to use fresh vegetables and fruits, keep in mind that most will keep in the refrigerator from two to five days and that you will begin to use them almost immediately. Shop accordingly.

Buy a large and varied assortment initially. Only you can estimate quantities, but a good rule of thumb is to take home just a little more than you think you'll need — but not so much more that they'll deteriorate before you get around to eating them. Shop again on Day 3 or 4, if necessary, so you'll have enough to finish the diet.

Pick of the Crop I — Best New Cabbage Soup Diet Veggies and How to Buy Them

The United States Department of Agriculture (USDA) is the ultimate expert on shopping for vegetables (and fruits). The agency offers these general pointers on buying the best.

• As a rule, the freshest vegetables offer the best nutritional value. Freshness in vegetables is indicated by bright, lively colour, crispness, and firm, rather than limp or soft texture.

• Don't buy just because the price is low. Though most produce is priced lowest when it's in season and theoretically at its best, low price sometimes goes hand in hand with poor quality or deterioration.

• Avoid decaying produce no matter how low the cost. Though you may be able to trim off the bad parts, rapid deterioration is likely to spread to the salvaged areas.

The vegetables on the list below are 'free' vegetables. This means that you can have unlimited amounts of them on Days 2, 3, 6, and 7 of the New Cabbage Soup Diet. They're low in calories and high in important nutrients. Vegetables not on the list have been omitted because they're too high in calories, too starchy, or are typically cooked with oil or seasonings that add significantly to their calorie content.

★ Important ★

If you are making a shopping list, be sure to include the veggies you'll need to cook the cabbage soup:
1 head cabbage
6 carrots
6 medium onions
6 spring onions
2 green or red peppers
3 whole tomatoes, or 1 28-ounce can of tomatoes
5 stalks celery

Now select as many different vegetables as you like from the list below. Choose a variety of leafy green vegetables; they'll help boost the calcium content of the diet. Important: Shopping tips for potatoes are included in the list below. However, potatoes are not free vegetables; you may have only one on Day 2 of the diet.

Artichokes (1 medium, 60 calories) Look for plump globe-shaped artichokes that are heavy for their size. The leaves (more correctly called scales) should be compact (not spread out) thick, green, and fresh-looking. Avoid artichokes with spreading leaves (an indication of toughness and dryness), areas of brown or greyish discolouration, and mould growth.

★ Note ★

Steamed artichoke leaves seasoned with a little lemon juice are good for nibbling anytime.

Asparagus (6 medium spears, 22 calories) The tips of these vegetables should be closed and compact, and the spears should be round, smooth, and green almost to the ends. Avoid tips that are open or spread out and 'ribbed' spears: both indicate age and toughness.

Beans (green) (½ cup sliced, 22 calories) The best are firm and crisp, with a bright green colour. Avoid wilted, flabby beans and those with thick, fibrous pods.

Beetroot (½ cup, sliced, 37 calories) Choose beets that are firm and round, with a slender main root, and a deep red colour over most of the surface. When beets are sold in a bunch, with the tops still on, look for leaves that are fresh and in good condition. Avoid very large, misshapen beetroots, wilted or soft specimens, and those with scaly surface areas.

Broccoli (1 medium stalk, 50 calories) Look for compact, closed buds. The colour of fresh, top-quality broccoli can range from dark, rich green, to sage green, to green with a purplish cast. Avoid yellowish green broccoli, buds that are enlarged or open, and specimens with soft or slippery spots on the bud clusters.

Brussels sprouts (½ cup, 30 calories) The freshest and best are a bright green colour, firm, and have tight-fitting outer leaves. Avoid soft sprouts and those with loose, wilted outer leaves.

Cabbage (1 cup shredded or sliced, 33 calories) Smooth-leaved cabbage is sold as new cabbage and storage cabbage (the latter are cabbages grown in the autumn and held for winter sale). Select the firmest heads of new cabbage. Leaves should be green and reasonably free of blemishes. Outer leaves, called 'wrapper leaves,' are typically loose on new cabbage. Avoid wilted or yellow leaves and specimens with many loose wrapper leaves; they're 'waste', as you will be discarding them before you cook the cabbage. Storage cabbage is usually trimmed of outer leaves and of a paler green colour. Avoid specimens with dried or discoloured areas and outer leaf stems that have separated from the central stem at the base of the head.

Carrots (½ cup, sliced, 35 calories) Select bright orange, smooth, firm, well-formed carrots. Avoid soft, flabby carrots.

Cauliflower (½ cup florets, 14 calories) Look for white or creamy white, solid, clean curds (that's the white, edible portion). Avoid softening, spreading, wilting, or discolouration of the curd, and specimens with a smudgy, speckled appearance.

Celery (1 cup sliced, 19 calories) Buy solid, crisp stalks, light to medium green, with a glossy surface. Leaflets should be fresh-looking or only very slightly wilted. Avoid celery with soft or flabby upper branches and stalks. Though celery that is less than firm and crisp can be freshened slightly by placing cut stalks in water, this procedure won't help badly wilted celery.

Cucumbers (7 slices, 4 calories) Shop for cucumbers that are uniformly green and firm. Avoid overgrown cucumbers and those with a large diameter. Withered or shrivelled ends signify toughness and bitter flavour.

Greens, leafy (1 cup, broken or chopped, approximately 15 calories. This is an average; different varieties deliver somewhat fewer or more calories.) Vegetables in this group include spinach, kale, endive, chard, cress, chicory, and sorrell as well as turnip, beet, mustard, dandelion, and other greens. Select leaves that are fresh, tender, free from defects, and a healthy green colour. Avoid wilted or soft leaves and leaves with a yellowish-green colour or thick, fibrous stems.

Lemons (1 medium, about 17 calories; 1 tablespoon lemon juice, 4 calories) Look for lemons with a rich yellow colour and smooth rather than very pebbly skin. Pale, greenish yellow colour is often a tip-off that the juice is especially acidic. Avoid lemons with darker yellow or dull skin; these signs of age indicate that the lemon is dryer and less juicy.

Lettuces (1 cup pieces, approximately 8 calories; different varieties may contain somewhat fewer or more calories) All lettuces, including iceberg and Romaine lettuce, should have fresh, unwilted leaves, free of blemishes. Iceberg and Romaine leaves should be crisp. Other varieties have softer leaves.

Mushrooms (½ cup sliced, 9 calories) Look for young, small to medium mushrooms. In the freshest mushroom, the cap is closed and the gills (the rows of paper-thin tissue under the cap) are not visible. When gills show, they should be pinkish or light tan. Avoid older mushrooms with wide open, badly pitted or discoloured caps and dark brown or black gills.

Onions (Bulb varieties: 1 cup sliced, 60 calories; spring onions: 1 cup chopped, 32 calories) Select mature, bulb onions that are hard, firm, and dry and have flat (not protruding) 'necks'. Avoid sprouted onions and those with wet or soft spots. Spring onions should have fresh, crisp green tops. Avoid spring onions with wilted or discoloured tops.

Parsley (½ cup, chopped, 11 calories) Look for fresh, crisp, bright green leaves. Slightly wilted leaves can be freshened by trimming the stem ends and placing them in cold water in the fridge. Avoid yellowed or discoloured leaves.

Peppers, sweet, red and green (1 cup strips, 22 calories) Choose bright-coloured peppers with a glossy sheen and a firm surface. The best are heavy relative to their size. Avoid peppers that feel flabby or soft to the touch, those with punctures, cuts, or watery surface spots.

Potato (1 medium, baked, without skin, 145 calories) Potatoes are not free vegetables on the New Cabbage Soup Diet. You'll be having only one potato in the seven days you're on the diet but you may as well get the best. Look for a firm, reasonably smooth potato, free of blemishes, sunburn (a green discolouration visible on and just under the skin), and decayed areas. Avoid sprouted, withered potatoes as well as those with large blemishes and bruising.

Radishes (10 medium, 8 calories) Medium-size radishes of about an inch in diameter are best. Select plump, round, firm, bright red specimens. Avoid oversized, soft radishes and those with yellowed tops.

Tomatoes (1 x 2½ inch diameter, raw, 26 calories; 1 cup, chopped, 38 calories) For best flavour, buy locally grown tomatoes, which are usually allowed to ripen on the vine. Look for smooth, blemish-free, well-ripened specimens. Rich red colour and a slight softness detectable by gentle pressure are indications of ripeness. Avoid very soft or bruised tomatoes, tomatoes with soft, watery areas on the surface; tomatoes with sunburn (green or yellow areas near the stem scar); and specimens with brown cracks in the surface). Note: if only underripened tomatoes are available, place them in a warm area, away from direct sunlight for further ripening. Do not store underripe tomatoes in the refrigerator, as cold temperatures prevent ripening.

Turnips (½ cup cooked, 14 calories) The most widely available turnips have white flesh and a purple top. Buy small or medium-size turnips that are smooth, firm, and globelike in shape. Avoid blemished or very large turnips; the latter tend to have tough, fibrous flesh.

Pick of the Crop II — Best New Cabbage Soup Diet Fruits and How to Buy Them

No one particular fruit is a must on the New Cabbage Soup Diet. You can have as many different fruits — and as much as you like of any of them — on Days 1,3, 7 of the diet.

★ Important ★

Shopping tips for bananas are included in the list below. However, bananas are not free fruits, and should be eaten only on Day 4 of the diet.

The same general rules for buying vegetables apply to fruits, too:

•   The freshest fruits offer the best nutritional value. Bright, fresh colour is a good indicator of freshness in fruits.

•   Fruit that is unusually low in price is not always a bargain. Though prices tend to be lowest when the fruit is in season and most plentiful, don't forget that damage and overripeness also drive the price down.

•   Don't buy fruit with signs of decay, no matter how low the price. Though you may be able to trim off the bad areas, deterioration will spread quickly to salvaged areas.

Remember, with the exception of bananas, only the fruits listed below qualify as free fruits on the New Cabbage Soup Diet. Don't buy anything that's not on the list; some fruits have been excluded because they are too high in calories to qualify as 'free'.

Apples (2¼ inch diameter, 81 calories) Of the many varieties of apples, some of the best for eating fresh are

Coxes, McIntosh, Braeburn, Gala, Granny Smith, Empire, and Golden Delicious. Look for crisp, bright-coloured apples with shiny skin. Avoid bruised and overripe apples (these 'give' easily when you exert gentle pressure on the surface). Apples with small tan or brownish spots are okay if the rest of the skin is smooth, firm, and shiny.

Apricots (1 medium, 17 calories) Look for plump, juicy-looking fruit with uniform golden-orange colour. Ripe apricots yield to gentle pressure. Avoid very soft or mushy fruit (too old), and very firm, pale-or greenish-yellow specimens (immature).

Bananas (1 medium, 104 calories) Important: bananas are not considered 'free' fruits; you will be having them on Day 4 only. Shop for firm, bright yellow bananas with intact skin. (Bananas are at their peak of flavour when tiny brown specks begin to appear on the skin.) Bananas with green tips or skin that has not reached the bright yellow stage, will ripen in a day or so after you get them home. Avoid bananas with advanced freckling or bruised or cracked skin.

Berries (including blackberries, raspberries, and loganberries) (1 cup, approximately 65 calories, depending on the variety) Although these berries are different in size and colour, shopping guidelines are similar for all. Look for berries that are bright-coloured, clean, plump, and tender but not mushy. Avoid leaky berries (wet or stained areas on wood or fibre containers indicate the berries within are overripe or crushed) and berries with traces of mould or decay.

Blueberries (1 cup, 81 calories) Select berries that are plump, firm, uniform in size, and of a dark blue colour with a silvery bloom. Avoid soft, mushy, or leaking berries.

Cantaloupe (one-half medium, 93 calories) Buy melons with the following signs of maturity: a smooth, shallow scar where the stem used to be; thick netting or veining standing out in relief across some or all of the exterior; a yellowish-grey or pale yellow colour under the veining. A ripe cantaloupe has a pleasant characteristic aroma even when unsliced and yields slightly to thumb pressure. Avoid overripeness, indicated by advanced softening of the rind.

Cherries (10 medium, 49 calories) Look for glossy, plump cherries with very dark colour — from deep maroon to mahogany red to almost black, depending on the variety. (The exception is Ranier cherries, which are straw-coloured.) Avoid shrivelling, brown discolouration, and mould. Small areas of decay are fairly common but hard to see against the dark colour. Check for them carefully.

Grapefruit (one-half medium, 38 calories) Pick firm, smooth-skinned grapefruits that are heavy for their size. Avoid specimens with very thick skin; you can identify them by their pebbly, rough, or wrinkled surface. Soft, moist areas on the skin and a soft peel that breaks with gentle finger pressure are signs of decay.

Grapes (10 medium, 35-40 calories, depending on the

type) Choose plump grapes that are firmly attached to their stems. As a general rule, bright characteristic colour is an indicator of sweetness. Avoid soft, wrinkled, or leaking grapes and stems that are brown and brittle.

Honeydew (1 medium slice — about one-tenth of the melon, 45 calories) Select melons with a smooth, velvety surface, slight softening at the blossom end, and a pleasant characteristic aroma. Avoid melons with no 'give' and those with cuts, punctures, or large moist surface spots.

Kiwi fruit (1 medium, 46 calories) Shop for plump, unwrinkled fruit, light to medium greenish brown in colour. Ripe fruit yields to gentle pressure. Firm specimens are not quite ripe but will be ready to eat in a day or so if left at room temperature.

Nectarines (1 medium, 67 calories) Select plump, rich-coloured nectarines that have begun to soften slightly along the 'seam'. Bright-coloured very firm fruits usually ripen at room temperature within two or three days. Avoid soft, overripe fruits and those with cracked, bruised, or punctured skin.

Oranges (1 medium, 62 calories) Oranges are required by strict regulation to be mature when harvested, thus a greenish cast or green spots do not indicate immaturity. Buy firm, plump, smooth-skinned oranges that are heavy for their size. Avoid lightweight oranges, which may be short on juice and flesh. Rough, pebbly skin is usually an indicator of less flesh. Dull, dry skin and spongy texture are signs of aging and deteriorating quality.

Peaches (1 medium, 37 calories) Look for velvety, well-coloured peaches with smooth skin. Ripe peaches yield slightly to gentle pressure; underripe ones will ripen at room temperature in a day or two after you purchase them. Avoid soft, mushy, bruised specimens.

Pineapple (1 cup fresh chunks, 76 calories) Look for bright golden yellow to reddish brown pineapples with a pleasant, characteristic aroma and very slight lifting of the eyes, or pips on the rind of the fruit. Avoid green, unripened pineapples as well as those with discoloured, soft, or moist spots.

Plums (1 medium, 36 calories) Select deep- or bright-coloured plums that yield slightly to gentle pressure. Avoid hard, poorly-coloured, wrinkled fruits as well as those that are mushy.

Strawberries (1 cup whole medium berries, 45 calories) Select berries with a bright red colour, lustrous skin, firm flesh, and an attached cap stem. Medium to small ripe strawberries usually have better flavour than the giant-size ones. Avoid berries with large uncoloured areas, greater than usual numbers of seeds on the surface, and oversoft, leaky specimens.

Tangerines (2¼ inch, 37 calories) Shop for tangerines that are a lustrous, bright deep-yellow to orange colour. The loose-fitting skin of many mature tangerines yields easily to gentle pressure and this lack of firmness is not an indicator of poor quality. Avoid tangerines with punctured skin or soft mushy areas on the surface, as well as very pale or greenish fruits, which usually lack good flavour. However, small green areas on otherwise high-coloured fruit are okay.

Watermelon (1 cup chunks, 51 calories) If you are buying a cut watermelon, look for firm, juicy, bright-red flesh, free of whitish streaks, and studded with dark brown or black seeds. Avoid pale-coloured flesh and whitish seeds (these indicate immaturity). To judge the quality of an uncut melon, look for relatively smooth skin that is midway between shiny and matt. The ends of the melon should be filled out and rounded (not sunken), and the underside or belly of the melon should be creamy in colour.

Just a reminder: only those vegetables and fruits listed above are suitable for use on the New Cabbage Soup Diet. Produce excluded from the list are either too high in calories, or are palatable only when cooked in oil or combined with higher-calorie seasonings. In short, if it's not on the list, don't eat it.

What About Frozen?

Obviously, frozen vegetables and fruits can be kept for months, so if convenience and minimizing shopping time are especially important to you, your best bet is to stock up on a large assortment of frozen varieties on your first shopping trip. The calorie count and nutrient value of frozens are similar to fresh.

You may choose frozen versions of any vegetable or fruit listed — as long as it's frozen 'plain' — with no syrup, butter, cream sauce, or any other seasoning or ingredient that affects the calorie count. Frozen green beans are fine, for example, but not a frozen green-bean and corn mix.

To get top-quality frozen vegetables and fruits, examine the package. Don't buy packages that are limp, wet, or sweating; these are signs that the contents are beginning to defrost. Stained packages and those with ice clinging to them may have been defrosted and refrozen on the way from processor to supermarket. Though they may be safe to eat, they will not be as tasty as never-defrosted produce.

What About Canned?

As a rule, canned fruits and vegetables are about the same as fresh or frozen in terms of nutrients, but they are rarely as good tasting. (An exception is the canned, stewed tomatoes you may use instead of fresh for the soup. Though the flavour of canned tomatoes is very different from fresh, it's a good flavour in its own right.)

When buying canned vegetables and fruits, read labels carefully. Whenever possible, select no-salt or reduced-sodium versions. Don't buy anything canned with syrup or other ingredients that up the calorie count.

How to Shop for Low-Fat Chicken and Fish

The New Cabbage Soup Diet allows unlimited amounts of chicken or fish on Days 5 and 6. For optimal results on the diet, get the kind that is lowest in fat.

Chicken

As a rule, the younger the chicken the less fatty it is. You can't very well ask the age of individual chickens in the poultry department of your local supermarket, but you don't have to. The youngest chickens are the smallest.

Smaller boiling chickens are leaner than larger ones and have considerably less fat than the chickens sold as roasters. Even small chickens, though, have hunks of yellow fat inside; pull out the fat before you cook the bird.

Fish

Fish is lower in fat than most other foods of animal origin, but some species are less fatty than others. The least fatty fish are the species that have the whitest flesh.

White-fleshed, lowest-fat fishes
Halibut
Plaice
Haddock
Cod

Medium-fleshed, medium-fat fishes
Trout
Catfish
Tuna

Darker-fleshed, higher-fat fishes — avoid them!
Mackerel
Salmon
Swordfish

What About Tuna?

Obviously, fish from the white-fleshed, lowest-fat group

are the best choices while you're on the New Cabbage Soup Diet. If you are a lover of canned tuna, however, you may include it on Days 5 and 6 of the diet — but not in unlimited amounts. Have no more than one individual-size can of white-meat tuna, packed in water per day.

A Look Ahead

You won't have to remember how much of each kind of food to eat on the New Cabbage Soup Diet. You'll find food plans, what-to-eat reminders, plus tips and ideas for each day of the diet in Chapters Nine to Fifteen of this book. Be sure to read those chapters as you follow the diet.

In the next chapter, you'll find important information on mental preparation for this diet — and for any long-term weight-loss programme you might decide to try after a round of New Cabbage Soup Dieting. Losing weight is more than just a physical process. It involves beliefs and attitudes, too. Don't skip the following chapter. It will help you prime your mind for dieting. In fact, it could make the difference between struggling to lose pounds and inches and easy, effortless weight loss.

priming your mind

The New Cabbage Soup Diet is easy to follow. As we've seen, it's made up of a combination of nutritious, low-calorie, low-fat foods that taste great and induce your body to burn off the pounds. It's structured; you don't ever have to decide what or how much to eat because the plan is laid out for you in advance. And you can have unlimited amounts of many of the foods you'll be eating.

This diet gives you quick results that provide early, tangible signs of success, and these signs — a trimmer-looking body, a new bounce to your step, a new sense of lightness and well-being — in turn generate enough motivation to propel you forward, all the way to the end. As the diet quickly and efficiently rids your body of excess fat, you'll feel more upbeat and confident about losing weight than you've felt on any diet you've ever tried in the past.

But to lose every pound possible and to experience

optimal results, you must bring something to the table, too. That something is commitment. Motivation will come soon enough, after you begin the diet. But commitment must exist from the very first.

Of course you want to lose weight. If it wasn't high on your list of priorities, you wouldn't be reading this book. But wanting to lose weight isn't quite the same as being committed to losing weight. For instance, you might really want to lose weight, but perhaps you've tried so many times in the past that achieving your goal seems like an elusive and impossible dream. Or maybe you want to lose weight but you've never tried to diet because you've heard so much about how hard it is from other dieters. Or maybe you want to lose a few pounds but your real reason for going on a diet now is to put a stop to the nagging you get from other people — your wife or husband, your doctor, your kids, maybe even your boss.

When you are full of doubts, or your heart isn't really in it, you are not truly committed to the weight-loss process. In that case, following a diet — any diet, including the New Cabbage Soup Diet — is more difficult than it needs to be.

If you want to lose weight but your diet history, or other people, tell you it's next to impossible, or if your motives come from outside instead of within yourself — the techniques that follow can strengthen your resolve and turn your desire to lose weight into weight-loss reality.

Take Out a Contract for Success

There is emotional commitment and there is contractual commitment, but in any kind of commitment, there is always a promise, either implied or explicit. When you commit yourself to another person, as in marriage, you promise to do certain things and not to do other things. When you commit yourself to buying a house, you promise to honour the terms of the sale. When your application for a credit card is accepted, you promise to fulfill the obligations set down by the bank.

A genuine commitment to losing weight also involves a promise — in this instance, a promise you make to yourself to abide by the terms of the diet. But rather than simply 'think' the promise, get it down on paper. Yes, put it in writing for the world to see. That way, your agreement with yourself becomes more real, more binding, and more important than the silent promise that exists only in your mind. In fact, psychologists have found that a written contract is an effective tool for helping dieters and others keep the promises they make to themselves. Some believe that making such a contract is an important predictor of success.

The most useful contracts for starting a diet specify exactly what you intend to do and include small rewards or incentives at intervals along the way to the big payoff — which is, of course, achieving the weight-loss goal. It is also helpful to have the contract 'witnessed' by a relative or friend. Here's a model contract for you to use:

WEIGHT LOSS CONTRACT
Agreement Made With Myself
Beginning (give starting date) *I will eat*
in accordance with the New Cabbage Soup Diet until
(give ending date).
I will give myself a small reward of
(enter three or four small, nonfood treats) *at the end of*
each day on the diet. (Spouse or friend) *will read and sign*
this contract.

(your signature)
(spouse or friend's signature)

Pick Your Prize

The reward you choose to give yourself at the end of every successful diet day should be something pleasurable that you won't want to miss. Something that you will anticipate so much, it keeps you on track throughout the day. The thought of even a very small treat can keep you going, if you don't ordinarily give yourself permission to enjoy it. A few ideas to get you thinking: take a long, luxurious bubble bath, or a do-it-yourself facial. Go out to a movie, or watch that video you've been wanting to see. An uninterrupted half-hour with a good book is a great reward if you love to read but rarely make the time for it. If you have access to a pool and enjoy swimming, a half-hour in the water might be a terrific treat. Maybe just visiting with friends, or having free time all to yourself would be enough. If you're the parent of small children, you may need the cooperation of your spouse, another adult or a babysitter to enjoy rewards like these, but asking for help — and even paying for it, if necessary — is well worth the effort.

Giving yourself small rewards for every successful day on the New Cabbage Soup Diet is tantamount to 'success insurance'. In fact, it is so useful, the technique is included in each of the Diet Days chapters.

Self-Talk

Another valuable technique for strengthening your commitment to this or any diet is to 'talk to yourself' in positive terms. Of course, you needn't actually talk aloud. Thinking the words is enough. The idea is to replace negative phrases — such as 'I'll never be able to see this through,' or 'Stupid me, here I go again on another diet that probably won't help me' — with positive phrases such as 'I will follow this diet,' or 'I know I'll be successful this time.'

The self-talk technique draws on some of the principles of cognitive therapy, practioners of which believe that feelings spring from words and that what we say to ourselves and others greatly influences how we feel. According to the cognitive therapists, anxiety, doubt, and even depression, are in large part the result of using negative words and phrases in the continuing mental conversations we have with ourselves. In the same way, feelings of confidence grow when we use positive words and phrases.

If you doubt the effectiveness of positive self-talk, try saying to yourself 'I feel terrific' a few times in the course of the next ten minutes. Say it with conviction and a smile on your face. Then notice how your body begins to relax and your mood starts to lift.

Among the negative phrases to watch out for are any that include 'no', 'not', 'never', 'can't', and 'couldn't'. When you are aware of having said words like these to yourself, correct them immediately with a contradictory positive thought. Change 'I'm no good at following a diet' to 'I can follow a diet'. Change 'I've never had any willpower' to 'I do have willpower'.

Do the same thing when you realize you have been mentally downing yourself with phrases such as 'I'm a failure', 'I'm incompetent', 'I'm worthless', etc. In the opinion of many cognitive therapists, saying these things to yourself creates feelings of helplessness and hopelessness and does more than almost anything else to damage self-esteem. Negative words and phrases can also deepen — or lead to — depression, and depression can make you vulnerable to the temptation to 'self-medicate' the blues with food.

As often as possible, use the same principles in conversation with other people. The negative words and phrases we use to refer to ourselves in company are just as potent as the ones we use in our private mental conversations. In fact, they may be more damaging because in broadcasting our doubts and anxieties about dieting to the world, we also define ourselves as failures in the eyes of others.

Positive self-talk, like giving yourself a small reward at the end of each diet day, is so important, the concept is included in the seven-day diet chapters — only instead of talking to yourself, you will be writing positive thoughts in a journal.

Find a Cheerleader or Keep It to Yourself

Many diet experts cite the 'misery loves company' maxim in urging people who want to lose weight to find a community of other dieters to talk with. It's the theory on which some of the major commercial weight-loss programs operate when they give dieters the opportunity to meet regularly with other dieters. Talking about the diet experience, freely and without embarrassment, has indeed proven useful to some people attempting to lose weight. But there's a downside to support groups: not everyone has good news to report, and the bad news can be disheartening, especially to those who are just beginning a new diet.

There's a better way to get help when you are starting a diet and that is to find a 'cheerleader' — one person who is upbeat, positive, and 100 percent on your side. If you know anyone who fits that description, spend some time with her or him before you begin the diet. Talk about what you want to accomplish and how you are going to do it. Ask for positive feedback.

A good candidate might be someone you know who is also about to start the New Cabbage Soup Diet. Ask around. There is more interest in the diet — and there are more people who want to use it to lose weight — than you might imagine. In any event, pick your cheerleader carefully, because some people may do more harm than good. It's unlikely, for example, that someone with a long history of diet failure will be very supportive of your efforts. For obvious reasons, you should also avoid anyone of a sarcastic, cynical turn of mind.

What if you don't connect with someone who will be fully supportive and with you all the way? If you think about the principles of self-talk — the value of positive words and phrases and the power to harm of negative words and phrases — you'll understand why it's almost always preferable to engage in no diet conversation at all than risk the damage that can be inflicted by people who put a negative spin on your efforts. In short, the don't ask-don't tell policy is best.

Think One Day at a Time

The New Cabbage Soup Diet is meant to be followed for just one week (three days for the blitz version). At the end of that time, you should make an effort to improve your eating habits. You may return to the diet after at least two weeks have elapsed, or you might decide to switch to a longer, slower diet to lose all the weight you want to get rid of. Whatever your intentions, you'll be more successful if you maintain your commitment to a slimmer, healthier body.

Another enemy of commitment to weight loss, or any goal, is the feeling of being overwhelmed by the magnitude of the task. We think of all the time it will take, all the willpower we will have to exert, all the deprivations we must undergo. If we worry too much about these things, we may begin to wonder if it's within our power actually to accomplish what we set out to do. That can lead to procrastination, or in some cases to a decision to scrap the project. But even if we grit our teeth and decide to move forward, the feeling of being overwhelmed can make it harder than it needs to be. Especially if we continue to think of the job as a whole.

But something almost miraculous happens when we mentally break the job into smaller pieces. Thinking one pound at a time, or one day at a time changes our perspective and shifts our focus in ways that make the project more manageable. Think about it. Doesn't the idea of losing weight a pound at a time feel more achievable than the idea of losing 100 pounds? Doesn't thinking of staying on a diet one day at a time feel more comfortable than thinking in terms of weeks, years, or the rest of our lives?

A big job is always completed in pieces whether or not we view it that way in advance. We write a lengthy report one page at a time. We paint a house one wall at a time. We lose weight one pound at a time, and we stay on a diet one day at a time. When we make a conscious advance decision to break a project into smaller steps, much of that feeling of being overwhelmed goes away, and along with it, many of the doubts we felt about our ability to complete the project.

The one-step-at-a-time technique is similar to that used by so many of the twelve-step groups and has helped thousands of alcoholics, drug users and yes, even dieters, to move toward their goals. You will rarely, if ever, hear a recovering alcoholic who has attended twelve-step meetings express ideas such as 'I'll never take another drink ever'. Or 'liquor is no longer an option'. Instead she or he might say 'I won't have a drink now'.

To get all the benefits of the technique you must focus your attention in the present moment — not on the mistakes you made yesterday, or on the difficulties you might encounter tomorrow or the day after, and certainly not on the prospect of never again indulging in foods that are bad for you. If your mind begins to stray back to the past or forward into the future — at least where your weight is concerned, reign it in. Command it to stay in the present and see how much better it feels to live and control your weight in the here and now.

Commitment to the weight-loss process is the key to success on any diet. Now that you've read about the commitment-enhancing techniques in this chapter, the key is in your hand. But, as you know, techniques are just words on paper until you make a conscious effort to use them. So set your mind to these techniques, really give them your best shot. You won't know how helpful they can be until you do.

In the next chapter, focusing on the rules you'll need to follow on the New Cabbage Soup Diet, you will discover everything you need to know to be a winner at the losing game. Success depends on playing by these rules, so be sure to read it before you start the diet.

rules to lose by

Yes, you can lose up to ten pounds — or more! — in your first seven-day cycle of the New Cabbage Soup Diet, and up to five pounds on the three-day blitz version. But only if you follow the diet exactly. That shouldn't be difficult. You'll never experience real hunger because you can fill up on the soup whenever you want to. The food is good and healthy, and as you'll see when you read the next chapter there are many quick and easy ways to make it even tastier and more satisfying.

Still, this diet is more structured than many other weightloss plans, and it's strict in the sense that you must abide by certain rules. It's going to demand a lot from you, in other words. But think of it this way: the rules leave nothing to chance; you can't make mistakes on the diet if you follow them exactly. In fact, taken altogether these rules provide a kind of blueprint for success.

Rule 1
Get a Doctor's Permission to Start the Diet

Rule 2
Don't Make Food Substitutions

Rule 3
Don't Omit Foods

Rule 4
Eat Until You Feel Full and Satisfied — Then Stop

Rule 5
No Alcohol

Rule 6
Cook Chicken and Fish the Lowest-Fat Way

Rule 7
Have Vegetables Raw, Steamed, or Grilled

Rule 8
Don't Use Calorie-Laden Condiments

Rule 1

Get Your Doctor's Permission to Start the Diet
This is the prime rule for all dieters. It was mentioned first in Chapter One, and it's repeated here because it's so important. Be sure to explain that you plan to use the diet for seven (or three) days only, and will allow two weeks or more to pass before you start a second cycle. While you are discussing the matter, ask the doctor if she or he thinks it would be a good idea to take a multivitamin and

mineral supplement while you are on the diet.

Rule 2

Don't Make Food Substitutions

As you know, the New Cabbage Soup Diet is not just low in fat, it's also very low in calories. Calorie consciousness is in accordance with the latest thinking in nutrition: for substantial weight loss to take place, it is as important to consume fewer calories as it is to limit fat. That fact has been stressed throughout this book.

But despite the emphasis on calories in the New Cabbage Soup Diet, it doesn't follow that all calorically equal foods are equally good for promoting quick weight loss. Or that you can substitute foods delivering equal numbers of calories for the foods specified on the diet, and still achieve the same, speedy and noticeable results.

For example, a half-cup serving of fat-free frozen yoghurt dessert provides approximately 140 calories. Two medium-size apples come in at about 162 calories. Knowing this, you might assume that there's no reason not to snack on a serving of no-fat frozen yoghurt dessert — a 'diet food', after all — instead of two apples (or any of the other free fruits or vegetables on the diet). If you went with the yoghurt dessert, you'd even be 'saving' twenty-two calories.

No one can dispute the twenty-two calorie savings, but that doesn't override the nutritional differences between apples and yoghurt dessert. With the apples, you get vitamins and phytochemicals that contribute to your health and well-being. Just as important, you get some fibre, which appears to increase the amount of fat excreted by the body, and which certainly enhances feelings of fullness and satisfaction.

With fat-free frozen yoghurt dessert, you get approximately seventeen grams of sugars in the form of regular refined sugar, corn syrup, and other sweeteners. Sugars like these don't advance the weight-loss process, and therefore have no place on the New Cabbage Soup Diet. The frozen yoghurt dessert won't keep you satisfied for very long — in fact, as with many other foods containing refined sugars eating it may trigger an urgent desire for more. The frozen yoghurt dessert has the nutritional advantage in terms of calcium (20 percent of your daily requirement in a half-cup serving). But you will be getting that much calcium, and more, in vegetables and the skimmed milk or plain fat-free yoghurt you'll be having on every day of the diet.

The point, of course, is not to put down fat-free frozen yoghurt desserts — or any other food that is not a part of the New Cabbage Soup Diet. There may be times when a serving of frozen yoghurt dessert is an ideal snack or the perfect way to end a meal. But not when you are on this diet.

The same is true of dozens of other foods that are caloric equivalents to foods specified on the diet — but which do nothing to speed the weight-loss process. It would take most of this book to list all of these foods, and to explain in each case why you're better off avoiding them when you are following the New Cabbage Soup Diet. Having a blanket 'no-substitution' rule covers all bases. The surest, best way to get rid of unwanted pounds is to abide by this no-substitution rule and consume nothing that is not specifically mentioned as part of the diet.

Rule 3

Don't Omit Foods

Every food on the New Cabbage Soup Diet is there for a purpose. You won't achieve the same quick weight-loss results if you ignore or omit any of them.

The cabbage soup is a high-nutrition food that delivers lots of fibre. Fibre aids the weight loss by filling you up with a minimum of calories. Because the soup can be eaten any time and in unlimited amounts, it's a sure cure for hunger, should it ever arise on the diet.

Like the soup, the free vegetables and fruits provide important nutrients and fibre and are excellent hunger preventives on their own.

The chicken or fish on Days 5 and 6 help boost the protein content of the diet.

All those bananas on Day 4, when you are approximately halfway through the seven-day diet cycle, will help you cope with carbohydrate cravings you may experience at about that time. Bananas are important, too, because they provide a sweet change of pace and texture from the other foods on the diet, while supplying you with fair amounts of vitamin A, niacin and iron, some protein, and an abundance of potassium.

The different elements of the New Cabbage Soup Diet, and the way they all work together, will keep you feeling satisfied, help keep food cravings to a minimum, and most important, get rid of the pounds you want to lose. You won't get the same extraordinary results if you skip any of them.

Rule 4

Eat Your Fill — Then Stop

Rule 3 tells you to have some of every food included on the diet, but Rule 4 reminds you that this is not a commandment to eat enormous amounts of any of them.

For example, you must eat at least one serving of cabbage soup every day you are on the diet and you are also encouraged to use the soup as a hunger-blocker between meals or whenever you feel the need to eat something. But you don't have to eat huge amounts of the soup to keep the weight-loss process on track. Have as much soup as you want, but if one or two bowls a day are enough to make you feel comfortably full, there's no need to eat more.

It's the same with the chicken and fish on Days 5 and 6, and the bananas on Day 4. Have as much as it takes to keep you feeling comfortable and satisfied, but don't eat just because the food is available to you.

How much you eat of the free vegetables and fruits is also entirely up to you. You should have several servings on days when they are part of the diet, but you don't have to eat enormous amounts.

Of course, you will lose pounds and inches on this amazing diet no matter how much cabbage soup and free vegetables and fruits it takes to fill you up. But you'll probably feel full on less of these foods than you think now.

Rule 5

No Alcohol

Alcohol is not permitted on the New Cabbage Soup Diet. From ale to vodka, all alcoholic beverages contain unnecessary and 'empty' calories.

An equally important reason to avoid alcohol on this or any diet is its capacity to lower inhibitions. (For many people, that's its greatest appeal!) A single drink might loosen you up so completely, that your commitment and motivation to lose weight on this diet begins to waver. Next thing you know you may be having a second drink, and accompanying it with handfuls of nachos with sour cream or guacamole!

During the short time you're on the diet, try to avoid parties and other events where alcohol is served. But when making an appearance is a must, why not enjoy a sparkling glass of water with ice and a wedge of lemon or lime? Water is calorie-free and unlike club soda contains little or no salt. It's refreshing, it will give you something to do with your hands, and it won't lull that part of your mind that keeps you alert and motivated to stay on the diet.

Rule 6
Cook Chicken and Fish the Lowest-Fat Way
When it comes to chicken and fish, there are two things to consider. One is the fat content of the item itself. The other is the method of cooking. In Chapter Four you learned which chickens and fish are lowest in fat. Here, we're concerned about how to cook them.

First, use no fat in preparing these items. Cooking fat adds too many unnecessary calories: for instance, a tablespoon of corn, peanut, or olive oil has 124 calories and even though the oil is used only as a cooking medium, some of those extra calories will end up in your stomach. It's the same with butter, at 102 calories per tablespoon.

Grilling, roasting, steaming, and in some instances, poaching, are all good no-fat ways to cook chicken or fish, the two 'meat' items on this diet.

a) Grilling
Grilling is quick, easy if you have the right equipment, and imparts a special flavour to many foods. In grilling, food is cooked over heat; fat in the food, if any, is melted by the heat and drips down between the bars of the grilling rack. In effect then, this method not only requires no fat, it also defats the food as it cooks.

The Canadian Rule for Grilling Fish to Perfection
Cook ten minutes for every inch of thickness. You'll know it's done when the flesh turns from translucent to opaque and flakes slightly when you test it with a fork.

b) Roasting
This method of cooking without added fat is done in the oven, and typically takes longer than grilling. Use it for chicken, if you like, but don't attempt to roast fish.
    In roasting, liquefied fat can accumulate in the pan and soak into the underside of the chicken. This can be avoided by setting the chicken on top of a rack placed in the roasting pan.

c) Steaming and poaching
These are less popular ways of cooking fish and chicken without added fat, but they're certainly worth considering. Steaming or poaching fish is especially good since these methods can produce a wonderfully delicate flavour and flaky consistency that are hard to duplicate otherwise. There are special

utensils designed for steaming and poaching fish. If you don't own a fish steamer/poacher, you can get similar results by steaming fillets in an inch or so of water or cabbage soup liquid in a covered skillet. Add a few leaves of crushed fresh herbs for extra flavour. Check frequently to see if it is done.

Chicken can be poached in the same way. Place it in a covered skillet in 1½ inches of simmering water or cabbage soup liquid. Cover the pan and check frequently to see if it is done. Crushed fresh herbs added to the broth contribute more flavour.

Rule 7
Have Vegetables Raw, Steamed, or Grilled
None of these ways of preparing vegetables requires fat, so like Rule 5, this rule helps keep the fat content down as low as possible.

Raw veggies are easiest to prepare, of course. Scrub, dry, and cut them into bite-size pieces. Keep a selection in plastic storage bags in the refrigerator so they'll be ready whenever you want something crunchy and good-tasting. You can also have a selection of raw vegetables — crudités — as part of a meal. Serve with lemon juice, or dip them in plain no-fat yoghurt sprinkled with fresh chives, dill, or other fresh herbs.

Scientists now recognize that light cooking actually adds to the healthfulness of some vegetables, especially those that are high in fibre. The reason: fibre can 'trap' phytochemicals in the vegetables and make them less available to the body. Heat helps free them up so that you get more of the benefits phytochemicals confer. As a general rule, cook vegetables until they are slightly softened. You probably already know that overcooking destroys some of the vitamin C and other nutrients in vegetables.

Steaming vegetables is easy and helps prevent loss of nutrients that might otherwise be leached out by boiling water. A vegetable steamer that you fit into a saucepan of boiling water is the ideal tool, but if you don't own one, you can make do with a metal colander positioned over a saucepan. Make sure vegetables in the steamer or colander are not submerged in the water, but suspended slightly above it. Cover the saucepan and steam the vegetables until they are slightly softened. Check frequently for doneness; steaming can be quicker than boiling!

Grilling is a wonderful way to cook vegetables. The direct heat caramelizes some of the natural sugars in vegetables and the finished product can be delectable indeed. Although some cookbooks instruct you to brush on a little oil before placing veggies on the grill, you can get very good results without oil. Check frequently to avoid charring.

Rule 8

Don't Use Calorie-Laden Condiments

In Chapter Seven you will find ways to enhance the flavour of the foods you will be eating on the New Cabbage Soup Diet. Every flavouring suggestion in that chapter is low-cal and low-fat. There are many, many other flavour ingredients not listed there, and you may wonder about these. It's impossible to list every flavouring or condiment available, so be a label reader and follow these guidelines:

- Don't use condiments or flavourings that have more than 25 calories per tablespoon.
- If a condiment or flavouring has less than 25 calories per tablespoon, you can use 1 tablespoon of it once a day.
- If a condiment or flavouring has less than 5 calories per tablespoon you can use as much of it as you like.
- Don't use 'regular' dressings on salads. In this context, 'regular' means that the dressing in question is not labelled low-fat or no-fat. Regular dressings are made with too much oil and deliver too many calories. Regular Russian dressing, for example, has approximately 76 calories per tablespoon; low-fat versions have about 4 calories per tablespoon, so you can use them to add more flavour to salads or vegetables. Unfortunately, oil and vinegar dressing, which many people prefer over all others, has about 72 calories per tablespoon.

The sugar versus artificial sweetener question was addressed in Chapter One. To repeat: say no to sugar, and yes to artificial sweeteners if you like.

Follow these simple rules and you'll be right on track and headed for a visibly slimmer, trimmer body in less time than you ever thought possible. Remember, the diet is strict but it's not hard. You'll have to pay attention to everything you eat, but you'll have plenty of good, nutritious food to enjoy — more than enough to feel full and satisfied — and the results will be worth it. That's a promise.

ten bonus tips for better results

Now you know the rules of the diet and why they're so important. Don't break or even bend the rules. Think of them as being 'iron-clad' — the Eight Commandments of the New Cabbage Soup Diet. Success depends on following them to the letter.

The tips and suggestions in this chapter are different. They're not essential to losing pounds and inches on the diet, but they can be extremely useful. In fact, some of them are so useful that they'll come up again and again in Chapters Nine to Fifteen, the section of this book that takes you through the diet one day at a time.

Much of the information that follows is based on work done by weight-control experts and psychologists looking for ways to help people lose the pounds that threaten their health and make their lives less joyful. Other tips and suggestions grew out of the plain, common sense of successful dieters who discovered that certain approaches were helpful to them in achieving their goals, while other approaches seemed to make dieting more difficult.

Read them all. Make a special note of the tips that seem most relevant to you and the circumstances of your life — and remember that information in and of itself is useless until you apply it.

Tips for Taking Off

- Keep a diet journal.
- Pick a convenient time to start the diet.
- Shop ahead.
- Don't overeat the day before you start the diet.
- Have meals alone or with close family members only whenever possible.
- Decide how to handle family meals.
- Take a packed lunch on workdays.
- Know what to order when you must eat in restaurants.
- Be more active.
- Keep going — even if you slip.

Keep a Diet Journal
This might be the most important tip of all.

You'll need a journal to keep the facts straight. For instance, you'll be recording your starting weight and measurements in your journal so that you'll know at the end of your first seven-day cycle of the diet — or three-day cycle if you're using the blitz version — just how much you've lost in terms of pounds and inches.

Your diet journal should be more than just a

record-keeping device. It should also be a motivating tool — as useful to you in staying committed to your goals as the positive self-talk discussed in Chapter Five. In fact, writing in your diet journal is a form of self-talk, made visible in ink or pencil, in which you reaffirm your intention to stick to the rules of the diet, tell yourself that you're in control of your eating, and cheer yourself on.

There may be times during the diet, in fact, when you feel a little shaky about your resolve, times when you are tempted to eat a favourite food that's not part of the diet, times when you don't feel at all positive about your ability to lose the weight you want to lose. Never mind. Write as if you believe. As with positive self-talk, the strong, positive words and phrases you use in your diet journal will take on a power of their own. Those words and thoughts will affect your feelings and your feelings will affect your behaviour. In a very real sense, the positive phrases you jot down in your diet journal are self-fulfilling.

Obviously, the kind of diet journal we're talking about here is very different from a diary in which you confess your failures, vent your anger and frustration, and air your deepest, darkest fears — about losing weight or about life in general. Just as positive journal writing has the power to strengthen and motivate you, negative writing can undermine and weaken your resolve. However, it can be very helpful to write about close calls — times when you felt tempted to chuck the diet and go on a high-calorie eating spree, but didn't, for example. The fact that you resisted proves how strong and committed you are. That's something to feel good about, and give yourself credit for.

In the Diet Day chapters of this book, you'll be urged to write in your journal twice a day, once in the morning soon after you wake up, and again in the evening just before you turn in for the night.

Pick a Convenient Time to Start the Diet

With enough commitment you can start the New Cabbage Soup Diet anytime, on any day of the week. Still, you can make the whole process easier if you arrange to diet during a relatively quiet week, when your schedule isn't cluttered with a round of social or business engagements with eating as part of the agenda.

If you're a veteran dieter, you already know how difficult it can be to navigate your way through the holidays — or even through a single party or business lunch — without being tempted to have at least a taste of food you know is incompatible with your weight-loss plan. It will be even more difficult while you're on the New Cabbage Soup Diet, because of its structure. Although this diet offers plenty of food, and you'll never experience true hunger while you're on it, much of that food is not the kind that is ordinarily served at a dinner party or business lunch.

For some of you, the suggestion to pick a quiet week for dieting will seem impossible to carry out because you rarely have a quiet week. If that's your situation, and you really do want to lose pounds with this phenomenal quick weight-loss plan, consider changing your schedule to fit the diet instead of waiting to start the diet when your schedule permits. Given a few days' notice, you should be able to cancel or postpone most of the events that would otherwise interfere with diet success.

Shop Ahead

The importance of shopping ahead for the food you'll be eating on the New Cabbage Soup Diet was discussed in Chapter Four, but it's worth repeating now, when you are almost ready to start this amazing weight-loss plan.

The day before your first day on the diet, make a list of everything you'll need for the entire seven-day cycle. Do the same if you plan to use the diet for three days. In compiling your list, be guided by the master diet plan in Chapter Four. Keep in mind that many fresh fruits and vegetables begin to lose their freshness after two or three days in the refrigerator and buy accordingly. Quantities and amounts are up to you. It's safer, however, to get a little more — rather than less — than you think you will need. That way you can avoid having to run back to the shops when you suddenly realize the next day is a free vegetable day, but all you have in the fridge is fruit.

Don't Overeat the Day before You Start the Diet

Many people have an impulse to binge the day before they begin a new diet. It's almost as if the fact that they're planning to diet tomorrow gives them license to indulge in an orgy of eating today.

But resist that urge you must, if you want to lose as much weight as possible during the following seven days. Overeating on the day before puts you at a real disadvantage because your body will have to deal with the excess before it can get down to the serious business of burning off stored fat. You will lose pounds and inches no matter what you eat the day before Day 1 on the New Cabbage Soup Diet, but you will lose more pounds and inches if you eat moderately on that day.

Have Meals Alone or with Close Family Members Only Whenever Possible
Sounds unsociable, but you'll be lowering your risk of slipping up if you avoid other people eating other foods at mealtimes.

Listening to mealtime comments from others can be as risky as watching them consume your favourite foods. And believe it, mealtimes almost always elicit comments about food and dieting — especially if the people you are eating with know that you are trying to lose weight.

You can never be sure that some well-meaning person, knowing that you are on a weight-loss programme, won't try to make you feel good by saying that you don't need to diet and that you look fine, just the way you are. Or that she or he won't offer you a taste of something you shouldn't eat — 'just a tiny taste, it's so delicious.' Or tell you about the futility of diets in general. Or even attempt to seduce you into following their own favourite programme. Comments like these aren't helpful and can be downright demoralizing. If you can't avoid other people at mealtimes, be prepared by steeling yourself in advance against temptation and discouragement.

You can hardly avoid your spouse and children or housemates, though, so tell them about the diet before you get started. Explain what you intend to accomplish during the week, and ask for their help. 'Help' in this sense simply means that they won't disparage your efforts or try to tempt you to eat foods that are not on the diet.

Decide how to Handle Family Meals while You are Dieting

A decision made early on can prevent confusion arising out of uncertainty about who will cook what, as well as who will eat what. Don't — repeat — don't try to impose this or any diet on the people with whom you live. You are the one who wants to lose weight. If other adults want to join you, that's fine, but it must be their decision. (As for children and teenagers, the New Cabbage Soup Diet, as you know, is not suitable for young, growing bodies and should not be used by anyone who is still physically immature.)

However, if you are the cook and meal planner at your house, it may be possible for you to integrate the diet and family meals simply by augmentation. Offer the cabbage soup, as well as vegetables, fruits, chicken, or fish (depending on which day's plan you are following) to family members, but make sure there is plenty of other food for them to eat as well.

If someone else is the cook and meal planner, life will be simpler for everyone if you assume responsibility for your food and let others cook and eat as they normally do.

The actual course you decide to follow here is less important than arriving at an agreement that encourages consistency and follow-through.

Take a Packed Lunch on Workdays

The New Cabbage Soup Diet was practically made for people in work. Just ladle some soup into a plastic container, select raw vegetables, or fruit, cooked chicken, or fish from the fridge, grab some napkins and a spoon and fork, stow it all in a bag, and you're set. If there's a microwave at your place of business, be sure to warm up the soup before you eat it. It's a proven fact that hot meals are more satisfying than cool or lukewarm.

Know what to Order if you must Eat in Restaurants
The New Cabbage Soup Diet is not restaurant-friendly. Your choices are limited to the following:

• Green salad or plain vegetables on free vegetable days
• Fruit salad or plain fruit on free fruit days
• Grilled chicken or fish on Days 5 and 6

Think of these foods as your collective ace in the hole every time you must dine out. Even if they're not featured on the menu, practically every restaurant will fix you a portion of one of these foods and serve it to you plain, with no sauce or dressing. Most of the friends who ask you over to dinner will do the same if they know in advance that a simple green salad, fruit salad, or chicken or fish is what you want. (If they can't or won't accommodate you, you can always bring your own food. You won't be the first dieter in history who arrives at a party with dinner in hand.)

Of course, key your choices to the day of the diet. To be sure you order food that is permitted on the diet day in question, double-check the menu for that day before you leave the house. On Day 1 you can have unlimited amounts of free fruit, but no vegetables, for example. On Day 5 you can have as much chicken or fish as you like, but no vegetables other than tomatoes, and no fruits.

Be More Active

Just as you should get permission from your doctor before starting this or any diet, you should also check with her or him before becoming more active. We're not suggesting that you embark on a real fitness programme at the same time you begin the diet. But this is a perfect time to get into the habit of moving your muscles a little more, and a little more often than you normally would. The benefits flowing from just a little more activity far outweigh the expenditure of time and energy.

Indeed, increased energy expenditure is itself one of the benefits of being more active. Every move you make requires energy in the form of calories. Which is another way of saying that in moving your body, you force it to burn calories that would otherwise be unused. A very small increase in activity, of course, burns only very small numbers of calories, but over time the extra effort can make a difference.

The advantages of being more active don't stop there. Even a little bit of extra activity can help refresh and energize your body and your mind. It can help you refocus on your priorities. Many people have found that when they include a few minutes of physical activity in the morning, they're better prepared for the challenges of the day ahead — including dieting challenges.

In each of the day-by-day New Cabbage Soup Diet chapters that follow, you will find suggestions for being just a little more active. You will lose weight on the diet whether you use these suggestions or not. But by increasing your activity level even slightly, you can ensure that you will lose as much as it is possible to lose — and at the same time, make the process easier on yourself.

Keep going — even if you slip

Many dieters behave as if one slipup — a single ice cream cone, a few french fries, a piece of buttered bread — can undo all the good that previous days of dieting have accomplished. Convinced that all is lost, they go off the diet and back to their old way of eating. Worse, they decide that because they haven't been able to stick to a particular diet, they'll never get rid of the weight they want to lose; in a fit of self-loathing, they go off on a binge.

Practically every word in this book was written to help make the New Cabbage Soup Diet so easy to follow you won't have to deal with slipups like these and the self-destructive behaviour that often follows. In the real world, of course, some people do give in to temptation and eat food that is not part of the diet. If that should happen to you, try to keep in mind that a single transgression does not wipe out the effects of all your previous efforts. Where weight loss is concerned, one day on the New Cabbage Soup Diet is better than no day at all. Two days are better still. And in every case, continuing with the diet after a slipup is better than abandoning it.

So don't be too hard on yourself if your commitment lapses and you go off track. Don't say to yourself, 'It's no use, I can't stay on the diet, so I might as well go out and have all the food I want.' If you really want to 'punish' yourself for a small transgression, a better way to do it is to get right back on the diet again.

It's almost time to start the diet. But before you do, take a look at the next chapter on how to give the New Cabbage Soup Diet more taste appeal. With the suggestions in that chapter fresh in your mind, you'll be ready to put more flavour into your meals — and get maximum satisfaction, along with maximum weight loss.

great taste!
how to make it
even more satisfying

You can follow the New Cabbage Soup Diet just as it was revealed in Chapter Three. That would be the Spartan approach. It's a perfectly good approach, similar to the one that has already helped thousands of dieters across the country lose the pounds that slowed them down, sapped their energy, made them look older, and most important, posed a risk to their health. The diet and the wholesome, nutritious foods it provides will do the same for you. As your body uses every vitamin, mineral, antioxidant, and phytochemical to help you stay healthy and feel terrific while the pounds disappear, these same foods, just as they are, will keep you feeling full and satisfied.

Without a doubt, some readers will prefer the no-frills Spartan approach for its ease and simplicity. There are people — and you may be one of them — who don't particularly want to enjoy food while they're on a diet.

They want to 'take' food, like medicine. But if you are in the majority and don't want to subsist on plain food if there's an easy alternative, there's a different, much tastier approach. You can make the New Cabbage Soup Diet and practically everything in it more enjoyable, and much more satisfying. You can do it in almost no time at all, with almost no extra effort. All it takes is some imagination, a few ideas for creating new food combinations, and for using traditional combinations at untraditional times, plus some no-calorie and super-low calorie herbs, spices, and other seasonings.

Taste Appeal

If you decide to take the more flavourful and adventurous approach, you'll be amazed by how much enjoyment and satisfaction certain combinations, and certain ingredients, judiciously used, can contribute to the honest, wholesome, and nutritious, but admittedly plain fare featured on the New Cabbage Soup Diet. In the pages that follow, you'll find ingenious ways to vary the cabbage soup and dozens of ideas for tastier breakfasts and lunches, along with suggestions for using foods in deliciously unexpected ways, and at unexpected times of day.

Add Zing and Variety to the Soup

Even without additional flavouring ingredients, the cabbage soup you will be having on the diet is a remarkably good vegetarian soup, as you will discover the first time you taste it. It's so good, in fact, that many dieters say they love it as is. Others want more variety, however, and the following ideas are for them.

★ Note ★

You can use these suggestions to season by the pot, or by the bowl. Seasoning by the pot — that is, adding flavour ingredients to the soup as it cooks — brings out richer, more fully developed flavour. Adding the same ingredients in proportionally smaller amounts to the soup after you've ladled it into a bowl gives you the opportunity to sample a variety of combinations over the course of two or three days. It's your choice.

★ Note ★

The amounts and quantities of flavouring ingredients in the 'recipes' below are approximations, erring if at all on the side of mildness. If you prefer highly seasoned food, just add more.

Cabbage Soup Italiano
½ cup chopped flat-leaf (Italian) parsley
2 cloves garlic, crushed
3-4 fresh oregano leaves, crushed, or 1 teaspoon dried oregano

Add all ingredients to the soup as it cooks; or use smaller amounts of each to flavour one bowl of soup.

Szechuan Cabbage Soup
2-3 thin-sliced spring onions
1-2 tablespoons soy sauce
½ teaspoon Chinese chilli paste.
Add all ingredients to the soup as it cooks; or use smaller amounts of each to flavour one bowl of soup.

Cabbage Soup Deutsch
2 teaspoons whole caraway seeds
3 sprigs fresh thyme, crushed, or 2 teaspoons dried
thyme
⅓ cup cider vinegar

Add all ingredients to the soup as it cooks; or use
smaller amounts of each to flavour one bowl of
soup.

Bengal Cabbage Soup
2 cucumbers, peeled and sliced
2 teaspoons ground cumin
2 teaspoons ground turmeric
If you have it on hand, saffron is a nice touch.

Add all ingredients to the soup as it cooks; or use
smaller amounts of each to flavour one bowl of
soup.

Tex-Mex Cabbage Soup
3-4 teaspoons chilli powder
2 jalapeno peppers, finely chopped

Add ingredients to the soup as it cooks; or use
smaller amounts of each to flavour one bowl of
soup.

Cabbage Soup Caribbean
1 teaspoon hot sauce
1-2 teaspoons ginger

Add ingredients to the soup as it cooks; or use smaller

amounts of each to flavour one bowl of soup.

Sweet and Sour Cabbage Soup
⅓ cup cider vinegar
1 packet artificial sweetener

Add ingredients to the soup as it cooks; or use smaller amounts of each to flavour one bowl of soup.

Savoury 'Creamed' Cabbage Soup
½ cup plain, no-fat yoghurt, or ½ cup skimmed milk

Add yoghurt or milk during the last five minutes of cooking time, or use a smaller amount to flavour one bowl of soup.

What's for Breakfast?

Many dieters had problems with breakfast on the original Cabbage Soup Diet, except on days when fruit is allowed. Fruit is still the ideal breakfast choice on Days 1, 3, 4 (bananas only), and 7 of the New Cabbage Soup Diet. But why stop at a single plain raw fruit? There are lots of other ways to enjoy fruit for breakfast. You can use all the foods on the New Cabbage Soup Diet any way you want to — as long as you don't exceed the suggested amounts (if any), don't add ingredients that contribute extra calories, and don't use foods that are not part of the plan for that day. Here are a few ideas that will give a scrumptious start to every day you spend on the diet.

Fruit Breakfasts for Free Fruit Days

Fruit Salad

Slice up your choice of fresh fruits, including watermelon or cantaloupe if you have them and combine them in a fruit salad. Fresh, ripe fruits are usually juicy and tempting enough without adding additional juice, but if your fruit salad needs more moisture or you prefer a very juicy salad, add a little juice squeezed from a fresh grapefruit or orange. Top it all off, if you like, with a sprinkle of cinnamon, nutmeg, or ground cloves. If the fruit is very tangy, you can sweeten it up by tossing it with some artificial sweetener.

You can't go wrong with any combination of ripe fruit (they're all natural go-togethers), but some of the most delectable fruit salad combinations include: blueberries and peaches; oranges, apples, and strawberries; pears and plums; watermelon, grapes, and kiwi fruit.

Fruit Salad Deluxe

To turn fruit salad into fruit salad deluxe, all you need to do is spoon ½ cup yoghurt into a bowl and pile sliced fruit on top. Subtract the amount of yoghurt used in the salad from your daily yoghurt allowance.

Going Bananas

On Day 4, when you can have as many as six bananas, enjoy at least one of them in the morning, at breakfast. You can have it plain or bake or grill it (see below), or float banana slices in ½ cup yoghurt (don't forget to subtract ½ cup of yoghurt from your daily yoghurt allowance).

Heavenly Cooked Fruit
Grilled fruit has an almost caramel-like flavour and aroma that is marvellous to wake up to, especially in winter.

Grilled grapefruit is a classic. It's as easy as placing half a grapefruit under the grill and letting it sizzle under the heat until the top turns bubbly and begins to brown. Sprinkle on some cinnamon and serve.

A few other fruits take to grilling, too: try the technique with sliced apples (slices should be relatively thick, not wafer thin); sliced peaches; sliced fresh pineapple; bananas sliced in half lengthwise.

Do not attempt to grill berries, melons, or any fruit that is very juicy (such as very ripe and juicy pears).

Baked Delights
Mention baked fruit and apples come first to mind. Baked apples, of course, are sensational. But apples are not the only fruit that take on a wonderfully different, more mellow, flavour when they are cooked in the oven. In fact, almost all fruit but melons, berries, citrus fruits, and other very juicy fruits can be baked. Set the oven temperature for 375 degrees and bake until the fruit softens and begins to bubble. Other fruits to bake are: banana, on Day 4, the 'banana day'; peaches, plums.

To bake peaches, plums, or other fruits with stones, halve the fruit and remove the stone before putting fruit in the oven.

Great Breakfasts for Non-Fruit Days

The bright flavour of yoghurt is a great morning wakeup call, and it's the perfect solution to the problem of what to eat in the morning on those days when fruit is not part of the diet. In fact, you might find that you actually prefer yoghurt every day on the New Cabbage Soup Diet.

Many people enjoy the tangy, refreshing flavour of plain, fat-free yoghurt, without other foods to dress it up. If you've never tried fat-free yoghurt in the morning, you may be in for a big, tasty surprise. Or, you might prefer to use the tanginess of plain yoghurt as a base and add 'top notes' with other foods. Yoghurt is a natural flavour complement to many vegetables, so there are dozens of possibilities.

Mix in fresh, peeled cucumber slices, then sprinkle yoghurt with chopped chives.

Have a yoghurt 'salad' breakfast on days that allow free vegetables. Just add to the yoghurt grated raw carrots, beets, and/or slivers of green or red peppers, and any other veggies that strike your fancy.

Potato for breakfast? Why not. On Day 2, when a baked potato is part of the diet, you can quickly microwave a potato, top it with yoghurt, and enjoy. Potato in the morning, of course, means no potato later on.

★ Note ★

Remember to subtract the yoghurt you have at breakfast from your day's allowance.

Delicious Ways to Munch at Lunch and Dinner

Lunches and dinners on the New Cabbage Soup Diet always include a serving of the soup. Have it plain, or try one of the variations given earlier in this chapter. The soup and a perfect piece of luscious ripe fruit (on fruit days) plus coffee or tea, may provide all the lunchtime flavour excitement you'll ever want or need.

Breakfast-at-lunch? At dinner? Why not? Here's where mix and match comes in. Though the breakfast suggestions mentioned previously are perfect ways to start the day, some of them are just as taste-appealing at midday or even in the evening.

Use these low-cal and no-cal ingredients to flavour-up New Cabbage Soup Diet Meals

• To add savoury goodness to vegetables, chicken, or fish, try: crushed garlic, cumin, curry powder, turmeric, caraway seeds, basil, rosemary, sage, thyme, dill, chives, parsley, sliced mushrooms. Fresh herbs pack the most intense and delicious flavour punch, so use them when you can.

• To add fresh, bright, or tangy flavour, try: lemon juice, prepared mustard, vinegar.

• To add a spicy bite to food, try: ginger, hot sauce, chopped dried peppers.

• To add, warm, mellow flavors that evoke a sense of sweetness, try: cinnamon, cloves, nutmeg

Lunch and Dinner Salads

Like fruit for breakfast, salad at lunch or dinner is an obvious choice — and it's an especially good one on the New Cabbage Soup Diet because the lively flavour and crispness of fresh, raw vegetables, dressed with a little lemon juice, low-cal salad dressing, or yoghurt is a wonderful complement to the mellower taste and softer textures of the soup. A simple lettuce and tomato salad is fine, but with the array of free fruits and vegetables you can have on this diet, you can pack a lot more flavour and variety into the meal.

A 'salad' can be almost any combination of vegetables, or fruits, so you can really be creative with all the free varieties you can have on the diet days that allow them. A few ideas to get you started:

• Crisp raw spinach, red onion rings, mushrooms, and sliced tomatoes.
• Mixed greens, including various lettuces, watercress, and a few leaves of chopped fresh herbs such as basil or rosemary — and grapefruit or orange sections.
• Coleslaw, made with grated raw vegetables such as carrots, beets, radishes, green beans, slivers of red or green pepper.
• The salad possibilities are unlimited — almost. It's important to use only those free fruits and vegetables listed in Chapter Four. Do not use fruit on Days 2, 5, and 6, the nonfruit days of the diet. Omit vegetables on Days 1, 4, and 5.

Grilled vegetables

You can make a side dish or an entire meal of a variety of grilled vegetables. Grilling brings out a delicious smoky flavour in the vegetables that is very different from the flavour of steamed. Some of the best vegetables for grilling are:

• Tomatoes, sliced
• Peppers, quartered, with seeds removed
• Large mushrooms, caps only

- Onions, sliced
- Zucchini, sliced into spears

Chicken and Fish

They're equally good for lunch and dinner, and on Days 5 and 6, you can have them at both meals. A few ideas:
- ½ chicken breast, drizzled with lemon and sprinkled with chopped chives or parsley, plus the soup.
- Diced chicken tossed with a low-cal salad dressing or a hot sauce-yoghurt dressing (yoghurt with one or two drops of hot sauce — depending on your heat tolerance) in a mixed green salad, plus soup.
- Grilled fish fillet topped with lemon slices, served with the soup and a side of grilled tomatoes.
- Flaked tuna with yoghurt-mustard dressing (three parts yoghurt to one part prepared mustard) and your choice of grilled free vegetables.

The suggestions in this chapter are just that — suggestions. Perhaps they'll inspire you to create new flavouring techniques of your own, or to come up with new mix-and-match meal combinations. In experimenting with new ideas, keep the following in mind:

- Don't use foods that add extra calories.
- With the exception of herbs, spices, vinegars, mustards, hot sauces, and pastes, and unsweetened fruit spreads, don't use foods that aren't part of the diet.
- Don't use fruits on nonfruit days, vegetables on nonvegetable days, bananas on nonbanana days, a potato on any day other than Day 2, or chicken or fish on days other than 5 and 6.

•   When you use yoghurt as part of a meal, or as the basis of a sauce, don't forget to subtract the amount from your day's allowance.

With these suggestions for flavouring up the New Cabbage Soup Diet still fresh in your mind, and with all the other tips and techniques in this book filed away in your brain, it's finally time to take off — pounds, that is.

day one

Here and in the next six chapters, you'll find menus and food suggestions for every day of the New Cabbage Soup Diet. Just as important, you will find dozens of ideas and tips — including simple ideas for getting more physical activity into your life — that will make the weight-loss process even easier. Some of the tips are specific to this diet. You can use them over again every time you return to the diet. Others will be equally helpful if and when you decide to switch to a slower, long-term diet — and for controlling your weight throughout the years to come.

Right now, though, before you begin the diet, read through this chapter and the six that follow. They'll provide a useful overview and give you a better idea of what's in store on each day of the diet. They'll also clue you up in advance on how to handle certain challenges — such as cravings, the need for 'food soothing' and boredom — should they arise. Then each diet morning, when you awaken, turn to the appropriate chapter for a refresher course.

If you are using the three-day blitz version of the diet, this is Day 1 for you, as well. Use the chapters for Day 1, Day 2, and Day 3. They'll help you look better at the beach, or slim down just enough to fit into favourite clothes that are now too snug.

The New Cabbage Soup Diet, Day 1

On the menu today:

Cabbage soup

Unlimited free fruits

1 8-ounce serving of skimmed milk, or plain, no-fat yoghurt

Tea or coffee, plain, or with artificial sweetener

1 tablespoon low- or no-fat salad dressing

Your choice of herbs, spices, and other low-fat or low-cal flavouring ingredients

★ Reminder ★

If you start the day with skimmed milk in your coffee, you are not permitted to switch to yoghurt later on in that same day.

Wake Up and Weigh In

It's a great day to start this diet so yawn, get up out of bed, and head for the bathroom scales. You'll be weighing yourself just twice on this diet — now, on Day 1, and once again on the morning after you complete Day 7 (or complete Day 3 if you are using the three-day version). To make weighing as accurate as possible, slip out of your robe, urinate, and then step on the scales before going in for breakfast. Record your starting weight in your diet journal.

Measure Up

You might want to take measurements, so that you can keep track of the inches you lose. You will certainly want a record of your measurements if you are planning to repeat the New Cabbage Soup Diet in two weeks or more after you finish this first cycle, or if you intend to continue losing weight on a slower, long-term diet.

You'll need a good, flexible plastic tape measure. (Don't try to use the metal kind; these are fine for measuring walls or windows, but no good at all for measuring the contours of the human body.) In taking measurements, pull the tape tight enough to eliminate slack, but not so tight that it presses into your flesh.

How to take Accurate Measurements

To measure your chest or bust, the tape should snugly encircle your upper back at nipple level. To measure your waist, draw the tape snugly around your abdomen at the level of greatest indentation. To measure your stomach, draw the tape around your abdomen at belly button level. Measure around your hips at their broadest point. Measure your thighs about eight inches above the knee (or wherever they are widest).

Journal Time

In Chapter Seven, you learned about the importance of keeping a diet journal — not just to record your progress, but to help you stay positive and motivated every step of the way. So right now, before breakfast, take time out to jot a few words of encouragement to yourself. Tell yourself how enthusiastic you are about losing weight on this diet and how you intend to make today a 100 percent success!

Breakfast Ideas

Day 1 is a fruit day. Since there's nothing like the crunch and juicy flavour of fresh ripe fruit for breakfast, have a selection of fruit, as many and as much of each as you want, from the free fruit list. Eat them as is, cut them up, and make a fruit salad — or a fruit salad with plain, no-fat yoghurt (see the fruit breakfasts in Chapter Eight for more ideas).

★Reminder ★

If you have yoghurt in the morning, you're locked into yoghurt for the rest of the day. The diet doesn't allow switching back and forth from yoghurt to skimmed milk. (Of course, you may have skimmed milk tomorrow, if you want it.)

Mini-Workout

Do some walking today, in the morning, if you can manage it. You don't have to walk very far or for very long, but you should walk more than you ordinarily do. A couple of ideas: walk around the block once or twice before you leave for work, or after you get there. (You don't need workout clothes for this, just comfortable shoes.) If a morning walk is inconvenient walk in the early evening for ten minutes or so.

Step out with your chest high, shoulders down, and tummy in. Keep the pace brisk yet comfortable. Take long strides and swing your arms.

Day 1 Lunch

Cabbage soup, of course, and as many free fruits as you want. This is a good day to have the soup plain, without any flavourful adornments. The soup is new to you now and you'll enjoy it just as it is. If you didn't pack it in a thermos, be sure to heat it up in the office microwave. Hot soup, remember, is more satisfying and filling than cold.

★Reminder ★

Eat alone if possible. That might mean having a solitary lunch at your desk. If you stay in for lunch, try to go outside for some fresh air when you are finished eating. Window shop, run errands, visit the library if there's one nearby, or just stroll. It's important that lunchtime on the diet gives you the sense that you've had a real break from your work.

Midday Slump?

Many people can practically set their clocks by it — that slowed-down, lethargic feeling that occurs at or about three p.m. each day. That slump is often accompanied by hunger and may be related to lowered blood sugar levels. However, if you had plenty of fruit at lunchtime, and your body is still making use of the natural sugar it contains, you may not experience loss of energy today.

If that slump does occur, have another piece of fruit (remember, you can have as much as you want today). The natural sugar in the fruit should bring your body's blood sugar levels back up again and see you through until dinner. This fruit prescription for midday loss of energy is a good one to use anytime — diet or no diet. The only exception is on nonfruit days of the New Cabbage Soup Diet.

Have the fruit alone, or with a jolt of caffeine. Coffee, as you know, contains more caffeine than tea, so if you are especially prone to caffeine jitters, have tea instead.

Progress Check

How are you doing so far? If you're like most people who follow the diet, you're doing just fine, thank you. You might even feel better than usual today — less tired, more peppy, and upbeat. Part of that good feeling certainly has to do with your changed eating pattern, especially if you ordinarily eat richer, fattier foods during the day. Rich foods load you down and can make you feel slow and groggy. Give yourself a figurative pat on the back for starting the diet.

Day 1 Dinner

Start with hot soup. You may want to try one of the soup flavour variations mentioned in Chapter Six. For dessert? You guessed it: fruit. If you're having skimmed milk instead of yoghurt today, you may drink all of it with this meal.

If this is a yoghurt day for you, there are several ways to enjoy it at dinner: You can stir some of the yoghurt into your soup to make it creamier. You can eat it plain or with the tablespoon of sugar-free fruit spread you are allowed on fruit days. Or you can have yoghurt as part of a fruit salad.

How to Increase Mealtime Satisfaction

You won't feel hungry on the New Cabbage Soup Diet

because there's always soup and, on most days, free fruits or vegetables to fill up on. You may occasionally feel unsatisfied — not because you aren't getting enough to eat, but because your food choices are limited and you can't have all the different foods you might want.

Physical and psychological satisfaction after a meal are extremely important to achieving the results you want on this or any weight loss program and there are several proven methods for getting what some people call 'more bang for the bite'. Put them all together, and satisfaction is almost guaranteed.

Slow down

Taste, chew, and swallow as slowly and deliberately as possible. It will give your taste buds a chance fully to 'register' the flavour and mouth-feel of the food. This is important because complete satisfaction depends almost as much on the experience of eating as on having enough to eat.

If you've been a fast eater all your life, you'll have to concentrate on slowing down. Try these techniques:

- Take a sip of water or skimmed milk between bites of food.
- Place your knife and fork or spoon back on your plate after each bite. Don't pick them up again until you are ready for the next bite.
- Chew your food thoroughly. Don't swallow until it is liquefied.
- If you are eating with your family or housemates, try to be the last one to finish. When you're alone, watch the clock. See if you can stretch your meal out to

a full twenty minutes or even a half hour.

Make meals special

Attractive food and a properly set table add greatly to the enjoyment of a meal; on the other hand, eating on the run, eating while standing in front of the refrigerator, eating while you're scanning the paper, can feel like no meal at all. Try to make your meals real.

• Don't eat without being seated at a table, with a place mat, plate, napkin, and silverware. These visual cues send a message to your brain that a meal is on the way. You may not have all the amenities when you're eating lunch at the office, but at least clear ample space at your desk, spread a napkin as place mat, and use real utensils instead of plastic.

• Don't combine eating with other activities. No TV, no book, crossword puzzle, or list-making — in short, nothing that comes between you and your food. (Soft, undemanding music, however, the kind you sense, rather than actively listen to, is okay, and will probably enhance your enjoyment.) It's important to keep your mind focused on your food. When your attention is elsewhere — and tasting, swallowing, and chewing become reflexive rather than deliberate — it's possible to finish a whole meal without it registering in your brain. You might even leave the table yearning for the meal you've just had!

Nonfood Treat Time!

Back in Chapter Four, you were encouraged to reward yourself with a small treat for every day you stay on the diet. Giving yourself a special, pleasurable experience in return for abiding by the rules of the diet can be an effective way to reinforce your commitment and resolve. Now's the time. Whether you choose a long, foamy, luxurious bubble bath or a quick visit to a good friend, don't skip it.

Bedtime

Today and for the remaining six days of the New Cabbage Soup Diet, you will be urged to write a few lines in your diet journal before turning in for the night. A diet journal, remember, is the place for giving yourself pep talks and pats on the back. (Be sure to date each entry and note which day of the diet you're on; you'll enjoy reading the journal in days to come.) Keep it positive. Congratulate yourself for sticking with the diet throughout the day. Tell yourself how easy it was, as well as how much you enjoyed the walking or other extra activity you engaged in today. Mention the times (if any) that you felt tempted to eat something not on the diet, but resisted the urge. End with enthusiasm for tomorrow — even if you don't feel that way. Getting it down in writing is a way to make the enthusiasm real.

day two

Welcome to your second day on the New Cabbage Soup Diet. If you felt marvellous yesterday, before you went to bed, you're probably feeling even better this morning: lighter, more energetic, full of confidence, eager to start the day and meet head-on every diet challenge that comes your way.

Some dieters, in fact, do find Day 2 the most challenging day on the diet because where food is concerned, this is the most restrictive day. Be sure to read this chapter through right now. That way, you'll be ready for all the diet-related challenges you might have to face.

Let's take a look at what you'll be eating in the next twenty-four hours.

The New Cabbage Soup Diet, Day 2
On the menu today:
Cabbage soup

Unlimited free vegetables
1 large baked potato
Tea or coffee, plain, or with artificial sweetener
1 tablespoon low- or no-fat salad dressing
Your choice of herbs, spices, and other low-fat or low-cal
flavouring ingredients
1 8-ounce serving skimmed milk, or plain, no-fat
yoghurt. You may have plain, no-fat yoghurt on your
potato if you like.

★ Reminder ★
If you choose this option, you must not have skimmed
milk today.

Wake-up Call
Don't weigh yourself this morning. Do spend a few
minutes with your diet journal telling yourself how good
it feels — finally — to be doing something about the
pounds you want to lose. You learned in Chapter Five
how important it is to approach any major endeavour
one step at a time, so think of today as your second giant
step to a healthier, slimmer body.

Breakfast Ideas
Fruit is the obvious breakfast food of choice whenever it
is allowed on the diet. Today, however, is not a fruit day,
so it's yoghurt to the rescue. If you like the tangy,
refreshing flavour of yoghurt plain, here's the perfect
opportunity to enjoy it. Otherwise, try flavouring your
yoghurt with one of the yoghurt-plus-vegetables
breakfast suggestions in Chapter Eight. If you want to
use yoghurt as a sour-cream substitute for the potato
you'll be eating later on today, make sure to save enough.

If yoghurt alone leaves you feeling less than satisfied and you want more food, heat up a bowl of cabbage soup. You'll be surprised at how satisfying it can be in the morning.

Mini-Workout

Before you get into the shower, do a minute or so of jogging on the spot, to burn off a few extra calories and to rev you up for the rest of the day. Music can help you get into the swing so turn on the radio and hunt around until you find something upbeat with an easy rhythm, or slip an upbeat cassette into your tape player. As you jog, keep your knees flexed (you want a loose, bouncing motion), bend your elbows, and pump your arms.

Eleven O'Clock Stretch

Many people need a short break at about this time in the morning. Stretching is ideal. It's pleasurable, relieves stress, and takes just a few minutes.

Try this: stand tall (if convenient, take your shoes off) and reach for the ceiling with your arms and hands. You want that stretch to 'open' the middle section of your body as it lifts your chest up and away from your abdomen. Try yawning. Somehow it adds to the enjoyment of a good, long stretch. How long you hold the stretch is up to you, but really try to get into it.

Now, if you have time, try one or both of these stretch variations. Stretch as above, but instead of standing flatfooted, go up on your toes and really reach for the ceiling. In the basic stretch position (arms lifted high, midsection open), shift your weight from one foot to the other. You'll feel a pleasant, alternating pull from your armpits down to your hips with each weight change.

Day 2 Lunch

Today you will have a bowl of hot cabbage soup and veggies, veggies, veggies. Some of you might want to have the baked potato you're allowed on Day 2 at lunchtime. Go ahead if that's your preference. Food choices on the New Cabbage Soup Diet are restricted, but there are no rules governing the time and the order in which you eat the various foods you are allowed.

Afternoon Pickup — The 'Ehhh ... What's Up, Doc?' Solution

Don't even bother with this section if you're feeling great and functioning in top form today. But if, like so many other people — on a diet or not — your energy level takes a dip some time in the middle of the afternoon, you may want something to eat now.

Fruit would be the best choice because of the natural sugar it contains but this is not a fruit day. However, vegetables with a high sugar content are almost as good. Chief among the higher-sugar veggies you are allowed on this diet are carrots, so why not use them to pick you up if you're feeling down? You can have as much as you want of raw, steamed, or canned carrots. Or you can have carrot juice — an even better choice because the natural sugar content is somewhat higher. Higher-sugar raw, steamed, or canned vegetables such as beets and parsnips are other options.

Have tea or coffee with your vegetable pickup if you want it. The caffeine in either can help boost alertness and energy levels in the middle of the day.

★ Reminder ★

You can have as much tea or coffee as you want on the

New Cabbage Soup Diet, but a word of caution is in order. Consume these caffeine-containing beverages in moderation. The diet is so low in calories and fat, that the caffeine in tea or coffee might have a greater effect on your body than it would otherwise, and increased feelings of tenseness and stress may result. That's just what you don't want now.

Day 2 Dinner — Flavour It Up

Dinner is soup, free vegetables with your choice of low-fat, low-cal salad dressing or other flavourings, plus that potato if you haven't already eaten it at lunchtime. You can also have coffee, or tea. If you decide not to finish your skimmed milk or plain, no-fat yoghurt now, be sure to have it before you go to bed.

★ Important ★

Why You Should Add Extra Flavour on Day 2
Remember that some cabbage soup dieters have found Day 2 to be more challenging than any other day on the diet. Day 2, after all, is the strictest day, with the narrowest range of flavours. Although you won't feel real hunger, because you can have all the veggies and cabbage soup you want, your taste buds, your mouth and your brain may not register full satisfaction with this narrower range of flavours. Since a variety of interesting and pleasing flavours helps keep your mouth happy, and your brain satisfied, this is a day to use plenty of flavouring ingredients in the soup and vegetables. Why not skip back to Chapter Eight and take another look at the soup and vegetable flavour variations it contains.

Nonfood Treat Time!

Sometime this evening, do something that you really enjoy. Anything at all is okay — except eating a favourite food. Back in Chapter Five you learned why: giving yourself a small treat at the end of each successful diet day helps you stay motivated and committed. As you progress through each of the next few days, you'll find yourself looking forward to the evening, and the pleasurable activity you'll engage in then. That spark of anticipation might help see you through any rough moments you might encounter on the diet.

There's another reason to give yourself a nonfood after-dinner treat, and that is to minimize feelings of deprivation. Psychological studies suggest that dieters who feel deprived and say to themselves 'It's not fair that I have to eat less than everyone else in the family', or 'Poor me, all the things I enjoy are forbidden', are less successful than those who come to terms with the fact that eating less of certain foods is a must if they are going to change their bodies and their lives. Your treat, then, is not just a reward; it's also a tool to help you avoid thoughts and feelings that can damage your chances for success.

Great Day, Good Night

Just before you turn in, get out your diet journal and jot down a few compliments to yourself. You've earned the accolades. After all, you've just come through the most difficult day on the New Cabbage Soup Diet — and you did it with flying colours!

day three

You're really feeling terrific today, not least because you navigated through Day 2, the most restrictive day on the New Cabbage Soup Diet, the day that so many dieters before you have found to be the most challenging one. You deserve every figurative pat on the back you give yourself. Nothing succeeds like success, and you've proven to yourself that you've got what it takes to achieve your goal.

You should be pleased with yourself even if Day 2 was in fact very easy for you. Knowing that you were able to do easily what others find difficult tells you how committed you are. And as you know, commitment and motivation are the keys to good results in weight loss — as well as to success in any endeavour you put your mind to.

Day 3, because it offers you more in the way of flavour and variety, should be a breeze.

★ Reminder ★

Read this chapter before you start the day so you'll be able to plan ahead in terms of food, treats, and the activities that will help you burn off extra calories.

The New Cabbage Soup Diet, Day 3

On the menu today:
Cabbage soup
Unlimited free vegetables
Unlimited free fruit
1 8-ounce serving of skimmed milk, or plain, no-fat yoghurt
Tea or coffee, plain, or with artificial sweetener
1 tablespoon low- or no-fat salad dressing
Your choice of herbs, spices, and other low-cal or no-cal flavouring ingredients
(No baked potato today)

Rise and Shine

Don't weigh yourself.

Get out your journal and record in black and white your positive feelings about yesterday, as well as how well you intend to do today. Tell yourself how proud you are, how strong and confident you feel, and how eager you are to get on with Day 3. Positive self-talk, remember, is one of your most important tools in successful weight loss. The principles of positive self-talk apply just as much to words and phrases you write in a journal as they do to the words and phrases you use in thinking or talking about yourself. So lay it on thick!

There will certainly be times on the diet when you don't feel 100 percent confident, and when you won't believe — at first — the good things you write about yourself in your journal. It doesn't matter. What matters is that you form positive words and phrases in your mind, and transfer them to paper. When you do that, amazing things happen. Your mind wraps itself around the words, the words begin to shape your feelings, your feelings start to change in ways that reflect the mood and meaning of your self-talk.

Breakfast

You can choose from the entire range of free fruits and vegetables for breakfast on Day 3, and you can have as many of them as you want. You can add plain, no-fat yoghurt to the fruit if you want to. And all the flavouring ideas in Chapter Eight are permitted. So enjoy.

★ Reminder ★

If you have yoghurt at breakfast, you are not allowed to switch to skimmed milk later in the day.

Mini-Workout

Some form of easy morning activity is important, so don't skip it. It will help burn off a few extra calories as it clears your head, warms your muscles, and sets you up for the day.

If the weather is fine, take a brisk walk around the block once or twice before you head off to work. Or plan to arrive at work a few minutes early so that you can do some walking before you get down to business. See if you can walk a little further and a little more briskly than you did on Day 1.

If it's raining, do some jogging on the spot. If you

were able to jog on the spot for a full minute yesterday, aim for ninety seconds today.

Whatever you choose to do, stop immediately if you begin to feel dizzy, have trouble catching your breath, or your body begins to protest in any other way. These symptoms are not unusual in people who are very overweight or unaccustomed to any exercise at all.

★ Reminder ★

The mini-workout suggestions are no more than suggestions. Don't feel you have to comply with them fully or limit yourself to the ones in this book. The idea is not for you to carry out these specific suggestions, but to do whatever you can to get a little more activity into your life.

★ Note ★

If you can manage a second round of activity at your office or workplace, or later on at home, so much the better.

Day 3 Lunch

As on every New Cabbage Soup Diet day, lunch should include a bowl of hot cabbage soup. If you haven't yet experimented with the flavour variations given in Chapter Eight, now is a good time to do so. The Italian version of the soup is especially tasty and so is the one called Cabbage Soup Deutsch (cabbage and caraway seeds were practically made for each other). You'll be surprised at how different — and delicious! — the soup can be when you add a few no- or very low-cal seasonings.

Have veggies raw or cooked just until they are

slightly softened. Finish lunch with a fruit dessert.

★ Reminder ★

Whenever possible, avoid business lunches that require you to have your meal at a restaurant. On days when you have no choice, order a fruit salad (on fruit days) or a leafy green salad (on vegetable days). Be sure to specify no dressing or low-cal, low-fat dressing.

Mentioning the Unmentionable

Sometimes, in some people, the vegetables and fruits on the diet, produce flatulence — gassiness in other words. Some of the most notorious of these gas-producing foods are beans, cauliflower, and — yes — cabbage.

Fibre is the culprit here. The problem seems to occur mainly when we consume the kind of fibre that is often called soluble, or digestible fibre. (Insoluble fibre tends to pass through the body without causing this annoying condition.) Soluble fibre is a component of the above-mentioned foods, and of many others as well. When these and other foods that are high in soluble fibre enter the large intestine, they are set upon by the billions of bacteria that make their home there. When the resident bacteria go to work, a few nutrients are freed up (most nutrients are absorbed earlier, in the stomach and small intestine) and waste products are produced. A by-product of all this activity is gas, with or without bloating or abdominal discomfort.

It's very possible that you will complete your seven- or three-day cycle of the diet with no gassy symptoms at all. If you are afflicted, however, there are ways to minimize and even prevent the problem.

How to Prevent Gas and Deal with it When it Occurs

• Get a head start on digestion by thoroughly chewing all your food. This will help break down fibre in the vegetables and fruit even before it hits your stomach. The more completely broken down digestible fibre is when it reaches your large intestine, the less likely you are to have trouble with it.

• Use a product such as Beano, a noncaloric liquid containing food enzymes that make fibre more digestible. These products are available at health food stores, chemists and supermarkets. Package directions instruct you to add a few drops of the product to the first bite of food. Don't add Beano or similar products to food as it cooks, since heat can deactivate the enzymes.

• Don't drink carbonated water with your meals. Carbonation produces air bubbles in the water, and swallowing air can contribute to the discomfort associated with gas.

• If you begin to experience a gas attack, try an over-the-counter product that helps combat indigestion.

Break Time

Treat midafternoon lassitude, if it occurs, with another serving of cabbage soup, or a fruit snack. If you choose fruit, select one of the sweeter free varieties listed in Chapter Four. An orange, ripe peach or plum would be ideal. Keep in mind that fruit that is not yet fully ripened contains less sugar and may provide less of the mood-lift and energy boost you want now. You may have tea or coffee with your fruit.

If you can leave the building for a few minutes,

take a quick walk around the block. It can do wonders to clear your head and refocus your mind. If you must stay indoors, try some long, lazy stretches, as described in Chapter Ten.

Day 3 Dinner

Have as much soup and as many free fruits and vegetables as you want. Day 3 dinner can be a veritable banquet because you are allowed unlimited amounts of all these foods.

For a real taste treat, try grilling an assortment of vegetables, including mushrooms. Grilling brings out a slightly different taste and aroma, while the mushrooms contribute an almost meaty texture to the mix. Be sure to slice vegetables destined for the grill into same-size pieces so they'll cook at approximately the same rate.

Nonfood Treat Time!

Once again it's time to reward yourself and reinforce your resolve with a small, but special treat. If you indulged in the same treat on Day 1, and Day 2, why not try something different this evening? The variety alone will help keep you happy and motivated.

The treat should be a top priority — more important than finishing household chores, paying bills or any of the minutiae of daily life that can get in the way of pure enjoyment. You need that treat, you deserve it, and except in cases of emergency, you should make the time for it.

And So To Bed

Even if you can hardly keep your eyes open, don't turn out the light until you write a few lines in your journal.

Congratulate yourself on a splendid Day 3, and make Day 4 even better by planting strong, confident thoughts in your mind right now, before you go to sleep.

Special congratulations if you're on the three-day version of the New Cabbage Soup Diet. You did it! And when you step on the bathroom scale tomorrow morning, you'll get your reward: more pounds lost than you ever thought possible in less than half a week! For even more gratifying results, you can, of course, continue with the diet. If you decide to stop tomorrow, wait at least two weeks before you start a second three-day cycle.

day four

In some offices, Wednesday is called 'hump day' because it falls in the middle of the work week, and it's all downhill until Friday. No matter what day of the week you started the New Cabbage Soup Diet, Day 4 is 'hump day'. It's the middle day of the seven-day cycle, and it gets easier, and more interesting, from here on in.

After three days on the diet, your confidence should be sky-high. You know you can handle the strictness and structure of the diet, and you feel good about the discipline and will to succeed you've discovered in yourself. Let these good feelings buoy you up and carry you on.

As for why the diet is characterized as being more 'interesting' from now on, one look at the Day 4 menu — as well as those for tomorrow and the next day — will clue you in.

★ Reminder ★

Be sure to skim through this chapter first thing today so that you'll know in advance what's in store for you where food, activities, and special challenges are concerned.

The New Cabbage Soup Diet, Day 4

On the menu today:

Unlimited cabbage soup

3 to 6 bananas

8 8-ounce servings of skimmed milk, or 7 8-ounce servings of skimmed milk and 1 8-ounce serving of plain, no-fat yoghurt

Tea or coffee, plain, or with artificial sweetener

Your choice of herbs, spices, and other low-cal or no-cal flavouring ingredients

All those bananas certainly are a dramatic departure from the foods you've been eating in the past three days. This shift in emphasis comes at just the right time. You've probably been eating more ripe fresh fruits and lightly cooked vegetables than you ever have before. But as delectable and healthy as they are, your brain and your taste buds may be crying out for something different now. You're getting bored, in other words. Today will fix that.

Up and At It

Pull out your diet journal, give yourself full credit for coming this far, tell yourself how committed you are to going the distance. Emphasize the idea that today's diet is different, and that you are really looking forward to getting on with it.

Breakfast!

Bananas. Have one or two plain, grilled, or sliced into yoghurt or skimmed milk. Some dieters like to mix a mashed banana with skimmed milk. They find that the resulting rich, smooth, thick — and sweet — puree is a welcome change of pace from the crisp textures of the vegetables they've been eating.

You must consume seven 8-ounce glasses of skimmed milk today (eight, if you're not planning to have yoghurt), so be sure to include a glass at breakfast.

Mini-Workout

If you've enjoyed the short morning walks you've been taking, keep it up. Just try to walk a little further and longer today and in the days that follow. You may need to set the alarm to go off a little earlier so that you have enough time to walk before you start the working part of your day — a horrendous suggestion if you are one of those who prefer to sleep as late as possible in the morning. Try to look at it this way: hard as it may be to get out of bed earlier, once you're up and around, those few minutes of lost sleep will be forgotten. And the feelings of satisfaction that result from doing something good for yourself — and important to the success of your diet — will make this small sacrifice well worth it.

If you prefer to stay indoors, do some more jogging on the spot today. Go for at least fifteen seconds more than you did last time. Skipping is another, somewhat more strenuous option. Try it if you feel up to it. Whatever exercise you choose for starting the day, see if you can arrange to repeat the activity later in the day, either at work or when you are back home in the evening.

★ Reminder ★

Shortness of breath, feelings of dizziness and any muscular or other discomfort are important signals from your body telling you to stop immediately.

Day 4 Lunch

Start with a bowl of hot cabbage soup, then have one or two bananas. It's not easy carrying cooked bananas from home, so if today is a workday, your best bet is to bring raw bananas and peel and eat them at lunchtime. Take a few moments to really savour their smooth texture and unique flavour. Bananas really are different from the other foods you've been having on the diet, so give your taste buds and brain plenty of time to register the difference. Finish with one or two 8-ounce glasses of skimmed milk.

★ Note ★

You'll be happy to know that bananas are much easier to digest than the vegetables and fruits called for by the diet up until now: many babies are introduced to solid foods in the form of mashed bananas because they're so digestible. For the same reason, the very old and the very ailing are usually able to tolerate bananas better than other solid foods. (In fact, it has been said of bananas that they're the first and last real food a person ever gets.) What does this greater digestibility mean for you? Simply that eating easy-to-digest bananas should eliminate much of the gassiness — caused by the abundance of foods containing harder to digest fibre — that may have bothered you yesterday and the day before.

Three p.m. and All's Well

The sugars in your lunchtime bananas will probably keep you feeling awake and alert for the rest of the afternoon. However, everyone is different in terms of constitution as well as energy demands and output, so if your spirits and vitality start to wane, have a bowl of hot cabbage soup, a banana, a glass of skimmed milk, or all three to perk you up in the middle of the day.

★ Note ★

Skimmed milk is most refreshing and satisfying when drunk icy cold. If you brought yours from home and haven't refrigerated it, you can make it more enjoyable simply by adding an ice cube. Try it if your office is equipped with a mini-fridge with ice tray.

★ Reminder ★

Caffeine, of course, can be invaluable as a mid-afternoon pickup (people don't go on coffee or tea breaks at this time of day for nothing). But don't have a caffeinated beverage if it makes you feel jumpy or on edge.

Stretching, jogging in place, or a quick walk around the block will provide an additional energy boost now.

What About Food Cravings?

It has been said many times in this book that you will never feel hungry on the New Cabbage Soup Diet, because you can always fill up on the soup, or on free vegetables or fruits when they are allowed. These foods are enough to keep most dieters feeling full and satisfied. But a few others feel hungry no matter how much cabbage soup, free vegetables or fruits they consume. You may be one of those others.

But is it really hunger? Probably not. More likely, what you are experiencing when you eat your fill of foods allowed on the diet — but still do not feel satisfied — is a craving for food. Hunger is what happens when your stomach is empty and sends out signals calling for more food. Hunger in extreme cases can be painful. Most of us are fortunate in never having felt true hunger.

Food cravings are sometimes linked to boredom or dissatisfaction. Often we crave something different to eat because we're tired of the same old thing. Other times we feel like eating something else because there's nothing else to do, or because what we're supposed to be doing doesn't engage our interest or attention. In those instances, what we really want when we say we are 'hungry', or crave food, is diversion — something to entertain ourselves with. If you think about your 'hunger' and decide it might actually be a symptom of boredom, change what you have been doing. Invent a different activity if possible. When the time and the place make it imperative to continue your present activity, at least recognize the 'hunger' for what it is — a craving. Knowing that dissatisfaction is probably a desire for diversion rather than food redefines it and helps you shift your focus from wanting to eat to wanting to find a more interesting use of your time.

True food cravings do exist, of course. Cravings for high-fat, high-calorie and high-carbohydrate foods are well documented. These cravings are often described as the brain's demand for nutrients from which it can make more serotonin, a natural chemical that helps ease feelings of stress and tension. Often, a small amount of a high-carbohydrate food provides the 'cure' for these cravings. A banana is high in carbs and can be useful in curbing cravings today. Cravings on other New Cabbage Soup Diet days may be harder to handle with food. High-sugar fruits can help, so reach for one on free fruit days. As for days when fruit is not a part of the diet, try managing your cravings as you would if they were generated by boredom: by finding something more interesting to do. Learning and using this technique has helped many dieters achieve success.

Day 4 Dinner

As always, cabbage soup is the entree tonight. Fill up on it, then have a 'dessert' of as many bananas as it takes to fulfill the Day 4 requirement. Dress them up, if you feel like it, with one of the ideas for adding more flavour to bananas in chapter 8. Unless you want to save it for bedtime, drink the remainder of your skimmed milk requirement.

★ Reminder ★

Check your cabbage soup supply. If you're running low, make another batch this evening.

Nonfood Treat Time!

Don't skip your treat even if today, with its infusion of new tastes and textures, hardly felt like dieting at all. Abiding by the rules of the diet, and being rewarded for doing so, helps keep you on track and fully motivated. For this evening, how about something that's not just fun, but a little outrageous or at least out of the ordinary? Something you wouldn't think of otherwise.

Such as bowling, roller skating, ice skating, bike riding, a few rounds of charades, twenty questions, Trivial Pursuit — you get the idea.

Sleep Time

Before drifting off, write a few lines in your diet journal. Tell yourself how easy it was today and how great it feels to take control of your food and your life. Then jot down a few confidence-building thoughts to sleep on.

day five

You're more than halfway through your first seven-day cycle of the New Cabbage Soup Diet now, and your confidence and motivation have been building since Day 1. The following three days (counting today), should be easier than the first part of the diet for several reasons: you've established a routine and have an idea of what you can expect from the diet, your body, and your mind as you go through each day. You're taking control of your weight and your life and it feels good — so good you don't ever want to lapse into your old, undisciplined way of eating and living. And the menus for the next two days offer you a range of interesting flavours and textures that have been absent from the diet until now.

If you are like so many others who have followed the New Cabbage Soup Diet before you, you're really ready for today's big food change. Just as yesterday's bananas may have given you the feeling that you weren't on a diet at all, the chicken and/or fish you will be having today might also make you forget that you are eating to lose weight. But that's exactly what you are doing. The weight-loss process is on track and proceeding full speed ahead.

★ Reminder ★

Read this chapter through before you begin the day. It will help you plan for the twenty-four hours to come, answer questions that might arise, and give you a handful of tips to make Day 5 even easier.

The New Cabbage Soup Diet, Day 5

On the menu today:

Unlimited cabbage soup

Unlimited fish or chicken

1 28-ounce can of tomatoes, whole or crushed, or up to 6 fresh, ripe tomatoes

1 8-ounce serving skimmed milk, or plain, no-fat yoghurt

Tea or coffee, plain, or with artificial sweetener

1 tablespoon low- or no-fat salad dressing

Your choice of herbs, spices, and other low-cal, low-fat flavouring ingredients

In Chapter Six, it was suggested that you choose the lowest-fat chicken and the leanest varieties of fish. Those guidelines are repeated here for your convenience.

Chicken

•   Leanest: smaller boiling and frying chickens

- Next best: chicken for roasting
- Avoid: capons

Fish
- Leanest: white-fleshed fish, such as halibut, haddock, flounder, cod, and plaice
- Next best: tuna, trout, catfish. (You may have one large serving of any of these today, in addition to leaner varieties. If you want to use canned tuna, choose the solid-pack white variety packed in water.)
- Avoid: darker-fleshed fish like swordfish, mackerel, salmon

★ Note ★

If this is a workday for you, be sure to pack enough chicken or fish to see you through lunch and still have enough left over for a quick afternoon pick up.

Good Morning!
Don't gear up for the day without writing in your diet journal. Give yourself more pats on the back. Make confident statements like 'nothing can stop me now'. Tell yourself how great it feels to be in control of your eating and your life.

Breakfast!
Today is not a fruit day, but who says the best days on the New Cabbage Soup Diet always begin with fruit? Fish for breakfast is a tradition in some countries, so why not have a grilled fish fillet — just as if you were breakfasting in an English country house, or out camping in the wild! Serve it with plenty of lemon juice to bring up the flavour. Another option: canned

solid-pack white tuna, also with lemon juice. If you'd rather have a fishless breakfast, choose plain, no-fat yoghurt. (See Chapter Eight for flavouring ideas.)

★ Reminder ★

If you start the day with yoghurt, you are not permitted to switch to skimmed milk later on.

Mini-Workout

Are you ready to add something new to your repertoire of morning activity? Try a little 'weight lifting'. You won't need real weights, just a straight-back chair and a couple of hardcover books weighing between one and two pounds each. Here are two easy exercises to get you started.

• Sit in a chair with your chest lifted, your back straight and slightly away from the back of the chair, and a book balanced on the palm of each hand. Slowly raise and straighten your arms until they are fully extended to each side at shoulder level. Bounce your arms (gently — you don't want to bounce the books off your palms) or simply hold in place for thirty seconds or as long as you can.

• Still seated in the chair with your chest lifted and your back slightly away from the chair back, grasp a book in each hand. Bend and lift your elbows, keeping your arms close to your ears. (Your hands, still grasping the books, should be positioned behind and close to the base of your neck.) Slowly raise your hands until your arms are straight and reaching toward the ceiling. Hold for five seconds, then slowly bend your arms until your hands are close to the base of your neck again. Repeat

five times. Try for more if you can.
• Finish your mini-workout with some jogging on the spot.

Day 5 Lunch

Lunch today is practically a feast. Start with a serving of hot cabbage soup. Go on to as much as you like of grilled, broiled, or roasted chicken or grilled or broiled fish. Add a large portion of sliced tomatoes.

If you've been wanting to have lunch at a restaurant, you can safely do so today or tomorrow. Just be sure to choose a place with plain grilled fish or chicken on the menu.

Eating with other people, remember, can be risky, which is why you were urged in Chapter Seven to eat alone as often as your circumstances allow. In addition to the reasons given there, there's still another rationale for eating alone: dieters and nondieters alike tend to eat more in social situations; they are especially likely to consume more food than they planned to when they eat with friends, coworkers, or other people whom they know well. One study, conducted by researchers at the University of Toronto, found that women volunteers (believing that they were participating in research on responses to the media — a 'catch a movie and grab something to eat' scenario) ate an average of 700 calories' worth of food. That was twice as much as what the control group of solitary eaters consumed. Forewarned is forearmed.

★ Reminder ★
No vegetables and fruits other than tomatoes today.

Quick Afternoon Pickups

It's very possible that you won't need food to perk you up this afternoon. That's because, if you have been following the meal suggestions for Day 5, your body has been supplied with an abundance of protein. What does protein have to do with it? Just this: because of its composition and the way your body digests it, protein helps maintain steady blood sugar (glucose) levels. When blood sugar levels remain steady, you are far less likely to experience some of the symptoms associated with low blood sugar, including lassitude, fatigue, and crankiness.

But what if you need a quick pickup anyway? Have a cup of tea or coffee. The caffeine should provide an almost-instant energy boost. You can also have more chicken or fish. They won't give you the same quick lift you'd get with sweet, ripe fruit or high-sugar vegetables, but the slower-acting protein in the chicken or fish will tide you over and keep you feeling alert for hours.

★ Reminder ★

Stretching, jogging on the spot, or a quick walk are terrific energizers.

Day 5 Dinner

Start with a serving of hot cabbage soup. Move on to more grilled chicken or fish. Have sliced tomatoes on the side or use them to make a sauce: it's easy. Just puree the tomatoes in a blender or force them through a sieve, add lemon juice, garlic, or dill, and your choice of other seasonings. Warm in a saucepan and pour over the chicken or fish.

Unless you want to have it at bedtime, finish your skimmed milk or yoghurt.

No dessert today. None of the foods permitted on Day 5 are sweet enough. But with all that high-protein food, you certainly won't miss it.

Nonfood Treat Time!

Remember, a small nonfood indulgence each day helps keep you from feeling deprived and unhappy. Plus, it's part of the promise you made to yourself when you started the New Cabbage Soup Diet. Keep it up.

Go back to one of the activities you enjoyed on previous diet days, or think up something new and pleasurable. If you're short on ideas, flip back to Chapter Five, where you'll find a number of suggestions.

Lights Out Time

As always, spend a few moments writing in your diet journal before you turn in for the night. Now is the time to flood your mind with good thoughts about yourself and the progress you are making. In a sense, those thoughts become 'concrete' when you put them down on paper. You might also enjoy reading some of your earlier entries. All of that positive self-talk will percolate in your mind and really set you up for Day 6.

day six

By now, you're an expert at following the diet. Your outlook is great and you are filled with energy —maybe even bubbling over with it. You're feeling lighter, there's a spring to your step, and you're ready for whatever Day 6 may bring. And it's all because you're learning how to manage your food intake and assume responsibility for your weight, and your life. You're on a real winning streak, so keep it going.

Where food is concerned, today, like yesterday, is one of the less demanding days on the diet. There's lots to eat. Including plenty of animal protein, which takes your body longer to digest and, like fibre, helps keep you feeling satisfied. Actually, today is even better than yesterday, because you can have your fill of free vegetables as well.

★ Reminder ★

Read this chapter from beginning to end so that you can plan meals ahead of time, and, if necessary, shop for foods you don't have in your kitchen now. It will also give you some problem-solving techniques to help you through difficult moments, should they arise.

The New Cabbage Soup Diet, Day 6
On the menu today:
Unlimited cabbage soup
Unlimited grilled chicken and fish
Unlimited free vegetables
1 8-ounce serving skimmed milk, or plain, no-fat yoghurt
Tea or coffee, plain, or with artificial sweetener
Your choice of herbs, spices, and other low-cal or no-cal flavouring ingredients

★ Note ★

Be sure that some of the vegetables you eat today are leafy greens. There's quite a range from which to choose, including: spinach, kale, mustard and collard greens, chicory, endive, and lettuces in all their endless variety.

Wake Up with a Smile!
It's a great day to be alive, and a great day to continue with the diet that is helping you lose more pounds and inches than you ever thought possible in just a week. Don't yield to the temptation of weighing yourself. Counting today, you still have two days to go. Instead, do what you've been doing every morning of the diet, and write some positive thoughts in your diet journal.

Tell yourself how marvellous you feel and how you know beyond a doubt that you are going to make this another successful day.

Breakfast!

Think in terms of a savoury breakfast featuring fish. Really flavour it up with your choice of fresh herbs such as dill, chives, or basil. For a nice touch, add some sliced or chopped onions. (You may add the onions to the fish as it grills; to prevent burning, wait until the fish is cooked halfway before you sprinkle them on. Just before eating, add the bright, tangy flavour of lemon juice.)

Plain yoghurt is always a breakfast option, so have it instead of the fish if you prefer.

★ Reminder ★

If you start out with yoghurt for breakfast, you are not permitted to switch to skimmed milk later in the day.

Mini-Workout

Walk, jog on the spot, repeat the easy exercises with weights you learned about yesterday. Whichever activity you choose, see if you can do it a little longer than you have in the past.

Doing Things the Hard Way

Today is also a good day to start burning off a few extra calories by doing ordinary things the hard way. The idea might seem counterproductive. After all, getting things done quickly with the least expenditure of energy is the goal in most areas of human endeavour. But it's different with weight loss.

Anything you can do to increase your level of physical activity will help you lose more weight more quickly on this diet or off. Anything. Walking down the hall to talk to a co-worker uses more energy — which is another way of saying it burns off more calories — than phoning. Standing up and reaching for a file placed high on a shelf uses more energy than pulling the file out of a desk drawer. Anything that can be done 'by hand' instead of mechanically — from mowing the lawn to sharpening a knife — will accelerate the weight-loss process. Of course, individually none of these small exertions will burn off more than just a few extra calories. But the accumulated effort over a period of days can make a real difference. Starting today, and continuing for as long as you want to lose weight or maintain your weight loss, try to get into the habit of doing things the hard way. In addition to the few examples given above, you can:

• Walk or bicycle to the store instead of driving or sending someone else.
• Rake leaves and pull weeds instead of having your spouse or kids do it.
• Get off the lift two floors before your stop and climb the stairs the rest of the way. Don't do this unless you are in good health.
• Hang the laundry out on a line instead of putting it in the dryer.
• When you're going to take the bus, walk past your usual stop and get on board at the next one.

The possibilities for burning more calories are practically endless, and you'll think of many more ways to incorporate the technique into your life. Of course, you will sometimes be limited by time constraints. Doing things the hard way often means doing things the long way. Nevertheless, the results over days and weeks will be worth it.

Day 6 Lunch

Today's lunch, like yesterday's, can be almost sumptuous. Start with a serving of hot cabbage soup, then have as much grilled or roasted chicken, or grilled fish as you like, as well as a salad of leafy greens and other vegetables.

Afternoon Blahs or Blues?

With all the high-protein foods you've been eating today, you may not need to recharge with a midday snack. If you do begin to feel draggy, have more chicken or fish, or some higher-sugar vegetables, such as carrots. Don't forget the instant lift you get from the caffeine in tea or coffee.

Stress Relief

Late in the diet, some people begin to feel stressed out. It can feel like hunger, it can feel like a food craving (they're different, as you know from reading through the chapter for Day 5). But often, the feelings of stress are linked to what some diet experts call the need for 'food soothing'. This need strikes particularly hard at those dieters who have learned to use food and eating to relieve stress, calm nerves, and reduce tension. Often, the longer the need for food soothing is denied, the stronger it becomes.

Calming with Deep Breathing

Deep breathing can bring you tremendous nonfood stress relief. Here's how to do it:

• With your chest lifted high, sit or stand up straight and take several deep breaths. Inhale slowly through your nose. As you inhale, concentrate on expanding your diaphragm — the muscular wall separating your chest from your stomach. Try to fill up that area with air. Don't gasp, puff out your chest or suck in your gut when you inhale.

• Hold your breath for an instant. Then exhale slowly through your mouth.

• The idea is to breathe in and out, a bit more slowly and deeply than you ordinarily do. If you do it properly, you can benefit from calming deep breathing anytime, anywhere, without calling attention to yourself.

• You might recognize the technique as the same one many performing artists use to calm pre-performance nerves. It will work for you, too. The effects are only temporary, of course. But you will discover that taking several deep breaths when the need for food soothing strikes will ease tension long enough to give you a chance to collect yourself and get your priorities back in order.

Day 6 Dinner

Begin, as always, with a large serving of hot cabbage soup. Have a main course of more chicken or fish. If you're tired of grilled fish, try poaching it. (The general principles are in Chapter Six.) Add free veggies, as much and as many as you like. Today, like yesterday, is dessertless, but by the time you finish everything on your plate, you'll be too full for it anyway!

★ Reminder ★

Finish your yoghurt or skimmed milk now unless you want to have it before you go to bed.

Nonfood Treat Time

Many dieters are most vulnerable to the need for food soothing on the last day or so of the diet, so this is the perfect time to get out of the house and into an entertaining non-food environment. If there's a ballet company, orchestra, rock band, stage play or sporting event you're eager to see, call about ticket availability. (Except for truly major events, you'll probably be able to get seats.) A long, lavish bubble bath is a natural soother as well.

Otherwise, repeat one of the activities that gave you pleasure earlier in the diet, or turn to Chapter Five for more ideas.

Ready for Shut-Eye

Get out your diet journal and applaud yourself and the progress you made today. Don't write about the fact that tomorrow is the last day of the diet. It's still too soon to anticipate the end. Treat today, instead, as just one more step in the process — one more day in which you behaved with confidence and conviction. One more successful day.

day seven

You probably woke up in a mood that is nothing short of triumphant. This is, after all, your final day on the New Cabbage Soup Diet, and you may have the heady feeling of a winner on a roll. No wonder: you are a winner. You've earned that natural high!

Perhaps you're surprised that just following a diet to its conclusion could make you feel this good. But think about it again, and you'll realize that what you are feeling is more than just the elation of having been successful so far into the plan. You're also feeling the excitement of being in charge and taking responsibility. You know that if you can do what you set out to do where dieting is concerned, you can do almost anything.

In some ways, this final day of the diet will seem familiar. That's because the food you'll be eating on Day 7 is essentially the same as what you had on Day 3. No more surprises, you've been through the complete food cycle and now you're almost back to where you started — minus up to ten pounds, and maybe even more!

★ Reminder ★

Don't start the day without reading this chapter from beginning to end. It's packed with tips and information that will ease you through the last day.

The New Cabbage Soup Diet, Day 7

On the menu today:

Unlimited cabbage soup

Unlimited free fruits

Unlimited free vegetables

1 8-ounce serving skimmed milk, or plain, no-fat yoghurt

Tea or coffee, plain, or with artificial sweetener

1 tablespoon low-fat, low-cal salad dressing

Your choice of herbs, spices, and other low-cal or no-cal flavouring ingredients

Wake Up and Write

You probably can hardly wait to step on the scales. But don't do it. The final results of the New Cabbage Soup Diet aren't in yet. Tomorrow morning you'll really have something to crow about. For now, reach for your diet journal and give yourself all the credit you deserve. Use positive self-talk and don't dwell on the thought that it's your last day on the diet. Write about your commitment to weight loss as if today is just one more step in the journey toward achieving the slimmer, healthier body you want for yourself.

Breakfast!

Naturally sweet and luscious flavours were missing from Days 5 and 6, and you're probably eager for fruit again.

Treat yourself to the freshest, ripest ones in the refrigerator. You're allowed as much fruit as you want, which means that you can enjoy two, three or more varieties. Have them separately or in a fruit salad, with or without plain, no-fat yoghurt. If you haven't yet tried grilled fruit, why not do so today? To enhance the natural goodness, sprinkle on a few grains of artificial sweetener after you remove the fruit from the grill tray.

★ Reminder ★

If you start out with yoghurt for breakfast, you are not permitted to switch to skimmed milk later in the day.

Mini-Workout

Walk, jog on the spot, give the easy 'weight' lifting exercises from Day 5 another try. Or just get up and dance. That's right — dance. Turn on the radio and surf the dial until you find music that makes you want to shimmy, swing, sway, twist, shuffle, hop, bounce, glide, whatever. Really get into it. Move your entire body, not just your feet and legs. Don't worry about what the kids, your spouse, or your housemates might think. Everyone dances in private once in a while. Dance as long as time allows or until you feel slightly winded.

★ Reminder ★

Yesterday you learned about the weight-loss advantages of doing things the hard way. It's more than just a good idea for dieters: it's a weight-control technique that can help thin people maintain their weight, and help everyone else control it.

Keep It Up

Do more exercise, rather than less, when you finish this cycle of the New Cabbage Soup Diet. Whether you plan to come back to this diet again (remember, you must wait at least fourteen days before you start the diet again) or decide to go on to a slower, long-term diet — or just want to maintain the weight loss you've achieved over the last seven days — exercise will help. Plan to make it part of your life from now on.

The super-easy mini-workouts in this section were designed to introduce you to the concept of being more active, to help ease you into the habit of including more activity in your daily schedule, as well as to burn off just a few more calories than you might otherwise. You will need to do a lot more exercise — especially of the aerobic kind — to attain true fitness and the health and weight-control benefits it confers and Chapter Sixteen will help get you started.

Day 7 Lunch

A serving of hot cabbage soup, and plenty of free fruit and vegetables is what you'll have today. Include yoghurt (if today is a yoghurt day for you), or finish with a glass of skimmed milk.

★ Reminder ★

Today's lunch can be as nutritious, healthy, and as filling as you want it to be since it allows you to eat as much soup, vegetables, and fruit as you want. Still, after two days of protein-laden lunches, today's midday meal might leave you with the feeling that something is missing. To make sure you get the maximum in terms of satisfaction and enjoyment, turn back to Chapter Nine and review the tips that help you get 'more bang for the bite.'

p.m. Pickups

If you need revitalizing this afternoon, have more fruit.
As you know, the natural sugars in fruit can help raise
blood sugar levels and quickly pep you up again. Try
tea or coffee for an extra-energy boost.

★ Reminder ★

If at all possible, stop what you are doing for a few
minutes in the middle of the afternoon and go outdoors
for a quick walk. Brisk movement is one of the best
antidotes for midafternoon energy drain. Stretching the
large muscles of your body is almost as good, so if you
can't get out of the building, try the simple stretching
techniques already described.

The Boredom Factor

The New Cabbage Soup Diet is designed for quick
weight loss, which is why it's made up almost entirely
of low-calorie, low-fat, high-fibre soup, fruits, and
vegetables, with a few other foods — such as skimmed
milk and yoghurt and the animal protein on Days 5 and
6 — to round it out. But by the time you reach Day 7,
boredom with this strict and structured regimen can
set in.

Boredom — with the food, with the routine, even
with the constant need to maintain self-discipline — is
one of the biggest challenges on this and other quick
weight-loss plans in which food is necessarily limited in
variety as well as calories. (Boredom can be a problem
even on a longer-term diet that includes foods from all
the food groups, but not as much of them as you have

been accustomed to.) These simple tips for coping with diet boredom will help get you through today and any day that diet boredom begins to get you down.

Shake up your schedule
Anything you can do to relieve the sameness and regimentation of other parts of your life will help with diet boredom, too. If you are at work, arrange to finish what you're doing and leave early, if possible, so you can take in a mid-afternoon movie, go for a drive, visit a museum or art gallery, or spend some unplanned intimate hours with your spouse or lover. If you've been shut up in the house, get out. If you've been keeping to yourself, seek company.

Get busy
Although it's not as much fun as sneaking off to a movie, or making love, tackling the things that need to be done is another way to banish boredom. Answer mail, make those phone calls you've been putting off, update your to-do list. If you're at home, reorganize a closet, put all those photographs in an album at last, clean out the garage. Any work that keeps your brain or your body fully occupied will also make time fly and take your mind off food and diet.

Try positive imaging
This is similar to positive self-talk, but instead of using words and phrases, you're going to work with mental pictures. If you do it correctly, escaping into a brief, very pleasurable fantasy can do away with boredom almost as well as the real thing. Here's how:
• Sit or lie down in the most comfortable position

you can manage. With your eyes closed, take ten deep, slow breaths. Try to make your mind a blank.

• When you are thoroughly relaxed, conjure up the most gratifying images of yourself you can think of. For many dieters the best thing imaginable is a mental scenario in which they are pounds slimmer and looking and feeling their best. Others prefer to imagine the realization of some other goal, such as a special career success, getting engaged, having a baby. Still others fantasize about being in the movies — even winning the lottery! The content of your fantasy is less important than its power to carry you away, so make the fantasy as vivid and detailed as you can.

• After five minutes, bring yourself back to the real world — but try to keep the excitement and pleasurable feeling of the fantasy wrapped around you as you continue with whatever you were doing before your session of positive imaging.

Day 7 Dinner

With a little creativity today's dinner, with its unlimited amounts of soup, free vegetables and fruit, can be a banquet. Start with a serving of hot cabbage soup, go on to a vegetable main dish and salad, finish with as much fresh, ripe fruit as you want. You'll find many ideas for flavouring each in Chapter Eight.

★ Reminder ★

Finish your yoghurt or skimmed milk now unless you'd rather have it as a bedtime snack.

Nonfood Treat Time

Just because it's your last day on the diet doesn't mean you can skip this important part of the weight-loss routine. As you are probably beginning to realize, doing something pleasurable as a reward for abiding by the rules of the diet does more than keep you motivated and committed. It also helps you recognize that you can have fun and enjoy yourself without resorting to food. That's one of the most important lessons you can learn on the New Cabbage Soup Diet.

Day's End, Diet's Over

You did it! It's the last part of the final day of this seven-day diet, and you came through like a champ. Congratulations. You probably feel like celebrating — and for good reason — but it's too late in the day for that, so reach for your diet journal and give yourself all the praise you deserve! Believe it or not, the excitement you feel tonight is nothing to what you'll experience tomorrow when you step on the bathroom scales.

The End and a New Beginning

Now is a good time to reflect on the diet, on your feelings about your seven-day success story, and on your future. Put it all down on paper, along with your intentions regarding further weight loss.

You have many options. Though you must end this cycle of the New Cabbage Soup Diet now because it's too low-cal and limited for long-term use, you can go back to it after two weeks or more of healthy, well-balanced eating. Or you might prefer to start on a sensible, slower-working diet that includes more food, and a greater variety of food, and use the New Cabbage

Soup Diet as a once-in-a-while tool for accelerating weight loss. Or instead of 'dieting', you can work hard at changing your everyday eating habits for good. More and more experts in the field of weight loss recommend the latter, and you'll find important information on how to make lasting changes in Chapter Sixteen.

The one thing you definitely should not do, if you care about your health and your weight, is go back to your old way of eating — the one that created the problem that made you try this diet in the first place. Have some of your favourite foods tomorrow if you want them, but promise yourself: no binges. No filling up on high-fat meals and snacks. Nothing that will undo the good results you've achieved on this diet. It shouldn't be hard. After all, you've already proved to yourself how disciplined and in control you are and you already know you're a success.

day eight
and after —
how to stay on track
now, and for the
rest of your life

Here you are, flushed with success on the day after finishing the seven-day New Cabbage Soup Diet. It's time to see what you've accomplished. Slip out of your clothes, step on the bathroom scale, and record your new weight in your diet journal. Check your measurements and record them, too.

The number of pounds and inches you lost has a lot to do with how faithful you were to the rules of the diet, and with how much you weighed when you started the diet. As a general rule, the dieters who are most overweight when they begin the diet shed the greatest number of pounds. The original version of the Cabbage Soup Diet projected a loss of seventeen pounds in a week. Those who actually did lose that astonishing number of pounds were often people who, when they started the diet, weighed sixty pounds or more over their 'normal' weight as it appears in standard height/weight charts. A loss of up to ten pounds — the amount mentioned throughout this book — is typical for women and men who were less than sixty pounds overweight according to the charts.

But whatever their starting weight, most people who follow the diet are not just surprised when the final results are in, they're elated. Some of them are so thrilled — and experience such exuberant feelings of confidence and motivation because of their success — that they immediately want to go back to Day 1 of the diet and start all over again. Maybe you feel the same way.

It has been said several times elsewhere in this book, but it is worth saying again here: you are not ready to begin another week of weight loss on this diet.

Your body needs a rest from this very low-cal, low-fat, high-fibre regimen. The New Cabbage Soup Diet supplies your body with many good, healthy foods. But as you know from having read previous chapters of this book, it does not give you adequate amounts of all the foods you need for optimal nutrition on a day-to-day basis. Waiting two weeks, during which you eat sensibly and consume ample amounts of foods that are in short supply on the diet, gives your body time to catch up. Then, and only then, can you return to the diet. During that interval, it's important that you start to change your eating habits so that you don't regain some of the pounds you've just lost.

In the pages that follow, you'll find guidelines on how to avoid weight gain between cycles of the New Cabbage Soup Diet or the three-day blitz version. With a few modifications, you can use these same guidelines to create your own slow, steady diet for long-term weight loss. This do-it-yourself diet will help you lose approximately one pound every week or ten days.

How to Eat to Maintain Your New, Lower Weight

It's axiomatic: if you don't want to gain back the pounds you have just lost, you can't go back to your old way of eating. The point is so obvious, it hardly seems worth mentioning, and yet many, many dieters — and not just the ones who have successfully completed the New Cabbage Soup Diet — fail to get it. They lose pounds and inches, then revert to the eating habits that made them overweight in the first place. When the pounds start to pile on again, they say the diet didn't work.

Most diets do 'work'. Meaning that if you are not handicapped by genetic factors that make you super-vulnerable to weight gain, almost any diet that supplies your body with somewhat fewer calories than it burns will result in weight loss. The New Cabbage Soup Diet gives you amazing quick results. Other diets will give you slower results. But no matter how you lose weight, you won't maintain the loss unless you change your eating habits for the better.

Nutrition First

Your first consideration when you are making food reforms should be to make sure you give your body all the important food elements it needs to function efficiently. It's not hard to do. Much of the basic information you need for good nutrition has been condensed and published by the United States Department of Agriculture in its Dietary Guidelines for Americans and Food Guide Pyramid.

You've probably seen the Food Guide Pyramid in

magazines and newspapers, or on TV, but for convenience's sake the recommendations included with the pyramid are printed here:

Each day
• Eat 6 to 11 servings from the bread, pasta, rice, and cereal group of foods
• Eat 3 to 5 servings of vegetables
• Eat 2 to 4 servings of meat, poultry, fish, eggs, seeds, nuts, or dried beans or peas
• Eat 2 to 3 servings of fruit
• Eat 2 to 3 servings of milk, yoghurt, or dairy-based food
• Fats, oils, and sweets should be eaten only sparingly

Portion Control

The Food Guide Pyramid seems to suggest that good nutrition requires us to eat huge amounts of food. However, a 'serving' is probably less than you think. The USDA definitions of a serving of various types of foods follow. These definitions will be useful to you in maintaining your weight loss as well as in creating a weight-loss program of your own.

In the bread, pasta, rice, cereal group, a serving of bread is one slice; a serving of cooked cereal, rice or pasta is ½ cup; a serving of ready-to-eat cereal is 1 cup.

In the vegetable group, a serving is 1 cup of raw leafy vegetables; ½ cup of other vegetables; ¾ cup of vegetable juice.

In the meat, poultry, fish, eggs, nuts, and dried beans group, a serving is 2 to 3 ounces of cooked lean meat, poultry or fish; ½ cup of cooked dried beans or peas. One egg or 2 tablespoons of peanut butter count as an ounce of lean meat.

In the fruit group, a serving is 1 medium apple, banana, orange, or other fresh fruit of comparable size; ½ cup of chopped, cooked, or canned fruit; ¾ cup of fruit juice.

In the milk, yoghurt, and cheese group, a serving is 1 8-ounce cup of milk or yoghurt; ½ ounce of 'natural' (as opposed to processed cheese); 2 ounces of processed cheese.

There are no serving sizes given for fats, oils, and sweets. Instead, go easy on the butter, margarine, gravy, salad dressing, sugar, and jelly you add to food in cooking or at the table, and choose lower-fat and lower-sugar foods from the other five food groups.

Cut the Fat

Just eating in accordance with the Food Guide Pyramid may be all you need to do to keep your weight stable between cycles of the New Cabbage Soup Diet. But you may want to go a step further. The following tips will help you reduce food fat on an everyday basis and insure against postdiet weight gain.

• Cook with less fat or no fat. This means grilling, steaming, poaching, or simmering most foods rather than deep-frying them. It also means using less fat in sautéing and browning. Frying pans with nonstick coatings are a big help here. They make it possible to sauté many foods with just a vegetable oil cooking spray. You may need to use some fat or oil to sauté other foods, or brown meats, but with nonstick frying pans, you can use less than you would if you were cooking in ordinary cookware.

•   When preparing foods such as pasta, stuffings, and sauces — from scratch or from a packaged mix — use less fat than the directions call for. In most cases, the dish you are making will taste just as good if you use only half the oil or fat specified in the instructions.

•   Use low-fat or skimmed milk in recipes calling for cream. Except when cream is necessary to create a thick, rich consistency, you'll get the same good results but with fewer calories. (Chilled, evaporated skimmed milk can even be whipped!)

•   Substitute plain, low-fat or no-fat yoghurt for sour cream as a topping and in recipes.

•   When you shop for meat, choose the leanest cuts. Trim all visible fat from meat and poultry before you cook it; discard the skin before you eat chicken or turkey.

•   Use little or no butter, margarine, salad dressing, or mayonnaise on vegetables and other foods.

•   Choose lower-fat versions of yoghurt, milk, cheese, frozen desserts, margarine, processed meat such as salami and ham, and other products. However, keep in mind that even those lower-fat foods can — and will — add weight, if you eat too much of them.

Go for Variety

Since different vegetables, fruits, meats, dairy products, and other foods supply different amounts, and kinds of nutrients, the Food Guide Pyramid suggests eating a variety of these foods. Everyone has a few favourites, of course, but make an effort to go beyond them. You might even discover some new favourites.

How to Create Your Own Customized Diet for Slow, Steady Weight Loss

Many people who attempt to maintain their weight by eating in accordance with the Food Guide Pyramid and using the fat-cutting measures listed above, actually begin to lose pounds. As mentioned earlier, the process is usually slow but it tends to be steady, except for those notorious plateaus when weight remains the same, sometimes for weeks at a time. In fact, another important use for the New Cabbage Soup Diet is to move you off a plateau (when you are on a long-term diet) and nudge your body back into weight-loss mode.

If you want to use the Food Guide Pyramid and fat-cutting tips as your basic diet plan — either for continued weight loss between rounds of the New Cabbage Soup Diet, or as a long-term diet in itself — you may need to adjust it so that it 'fits' your body and your food preferences.

How to Calculate Calories for Slow, Steady Weight Loss

To find out approximately how many calories you can eat and still lose weight at a slow but steady pace, the first step is to multiply your present weight by one of the following numbers:

14 — If you are sedentary
15 — If you are somewhat active
16 — If you are moderately active
17 — If you are very active

Many people sit at a desk for most of each day and make little or no effort to exercise when they are off the job. In short, they are sedentary. Let's assume that you are sedentary and that your present weight is 160 pounds. Multiply 160 times 14 to find the number of calories you need to eat each day to maintain your present weight: 160 x 14 = 2,240. In other words, 2,240 calories is the magic number that will help you stabilize your weight.

But you want to lose weight. That means you need to consume fewer than 2,240 calories each day. How much less? All else being equal, if you consumed 100 fewer calories a day, you would lose approximately 10 pounds a year. Consuming 200 calories a day less would result in a 20-pound loss over a year. And so on.

Of course, you need to recalculate as you lose weight. Let's say you started at 160 pounds and have lost 10 pounds over the last few months, but have not increased your activity level. To find out how many calories you can consume and continue to lose weight at the same slow rate, multiply your new weight, 150 pounds, by 14: 150 x 14 = 2,100. Twenty-one hundred calories a day is the new magic number to aim for if you want to continue losing weight at about the same rate.

These figures are only approximate and vary depending on whether you are a woman or man (women, in general, need to consume somewhat fewer calories to maintain and to lose weight than men), your bone structure, your metabolic inheritance as well as your age. Nevertheless, using the formula is a more effective way to calculate how many calories you need to maintain your weight or lose pounds, than making an uninformed guess.

★ Note ★

Many researchers in the field of weight control set a 'safe' daily calorie level for long-term dieting at about 1,200 calories a day for women, 1,400 calories a day for men. Some suggest consuming even greater numbers of calories. These experts usually advise dieters to boost activity levels rather than go below those limits.

Now you have all the information you need to create your own customized plan for maintaining your present weight or for losing pounds gradually over weeks and months. To put it all together:

• Use the Food Guide Pyramid as a model for good nutrition.
• Use the fat-cutting tips to pare away unnecessary calories.
• Use the formula for calculating the number of calories you need to keep your weight stable — or to lose weight slowly but steadily.
• Finally, adjust your food intake so that you are consuming the number of calories required for maintenance or weight loss.

How do you manage that? Use food labels to find calories per serving of packaged foods. Consult a good calorie counting book or other reliable source for the number of calories in fresh fruits, vegetables, meats, and other unlabelled products. (You'll soon know the approximate calories delivered by common foods well enough to dispense with the book entirely.) Eat less of the higher-calorie foods and more of the ones containing fewer calories. You'll discover when you try it that this method of creating your own weight-loss plan is a lot easier than it sounds — especially if you don't make a fetish of calorie counting. Exact calorie counting is unnecessary; approximations are fine.

More Ideas for Customizing a Diet

Where food is concerned, we're all different. We have different preferences and different styles of eating. A long-term weight-control plan — whether the goal is stabilizing your present weight, or losing pounds slowly — will be more successful if it works with your individual differences rather than against them. How can you change a basic food plan into one that's just right for you? Ask yourself the questions below and let your answers dictate how to tailor the plan to suit your needs.

Am I a nibbler? If the answer is yes, and you feel better and more satisfied when you can nibble between meals rather than limit your eating to three squares a day with several hours between each, then by all means, divide your meals into smaller mini-meals that you can eat at shorter intervals. Instead of having coffee, cereal, toast, and fruit or fruit juice for breakfast, for instance, you can have cereal and coffee soon after you get out of bed, enjoy your toast on the way to work, and have fruit or juice at 10 a.m. Other meals can be split in the same way. Your nibbling needs will be met, by consuming real food, not junk food.

What time of day am I usually most hungry? If you're one of the relatively few people who wake up ravenous, make breakfast your biggest meal of the day. More likely, your appetite grows as the day progresses. If your strongest desire for food comes in the afternoon, you can save most of your lunch to eat then. A late lunch, in fact, might result in a decreased appetite for dinner, which can be a good thing since we know that food eaten late in the day is more easily converted to fat than the same food eaten earlier.

What foods do I find most satisfying? Often, the answer is a food high in complex carbohydrates — bread, for instance, or pasta. For some people it's meat, or potatoes. Complex carbs, meat and potatoes all have a place in the Food Guide Pyramid hierarchy. You can emphasize these foods in your custom-tailored diet by consuming them in amounts that correspond to the upper limits suggested by the Pyramid. Example: the Pyramid suggests six to eleven servings of complex carbs; if these are foods that are particularly satisfying for you, have up to eleven servings a day of them — or at least enough of them to keep you feeling content and comfortably full when you leave the table. However, to keep calorie consumption within your target range, you may have to eat less of other foods, or be more vigilant about consuming less fat. The same is true of meat, potatoes, or any other foods that fall into your 'most satisfying' category. Eat more of them but cut back, if you must, in other areas.

What foods do I really crave? Where long-term, sensible eating is concerned, the latest thinking about food cravings is that you probably should give in to them occasionally. This applies across the board — even to rich or sweet foods, such as ice cream, fried chicken, or chocolate. Have a small amount. (Sometimes just a taste is enough to turn off the craving.) And of course don't indulge every day. If you do not give in to food cravings once in a while, goes the theory, the cravings may become so intense that you forget your commitment to sensible eating and go off on a wild food binge.

Put It All Together — Then Add Exercise

Diet books written as recently as fifteen years ago rarely mentioned exercise as an important adjunct to calorie cutting in the weight-loss process. When exercise was mentioned at all, it was usually in the context of firming flabby muscles, or defining a waistline, rather than as a way to lose pounds. Since then, studies measuring the impact of higher activity levels on nondieters and dieters alike have convinced researchers that exercise is an extremely useful tool in weight control. In fact, some studies seem to indicate that the healthiest, most permanent way to lose weight and keep it off is to engage in some form of physical activity for a half hour, several times a week.

It was suggested in the diet days section of this book that you try to get in just a little bit of extra physical activity each day. The Mini-Workouts in those chapters are not enough to make a major difference in calorie burnoff. However, they do get you moving — and all extra movement demands a small additional expenditure of calories. The Mini-Workouts also helped you become accustomed to the idea of setting aside regular time for exercise.

Keep exercising, even now when you're between cycles of the New Cabbage Soup Diet. A little extra activity each day is good for you on or off a diet. It will help you maintain your weight loss and buoy up your spirits. It will also prepare you for a fitness programme that will help you stay healthier — and slimmer — for the rest of your life.

Planning a Fitness Program

If you are very overweight now, you may have lost confidence in your body and your ability to engage in additional activity. The best antidote for this kind of insecurity is to speak to your doctor about the advisability of being more active. Assuming she or he gives you the go-ahead, here's how to get started.

• Pick an easy, enjoyable aerobic activity. Aerobic activity, which involves continuous movement of the large muscles of the body, conditions your heart and lungs. It accelerates fat loss and increases muscle mass. (This change in body composition actually helps accelerate the rate at which you burn calories.) And it also stimulates your body to produce more of substances such as glucose, serotonin, noradrenaline, and adrenaline, which are natural appetite suppressants and also help elevate your mood.

Walking is one of the best aerobic activities because you can set your own pace, you need no special equipment, you can do it anywhere, anytime, and it's sociable; with a walking buddy, time seems to fly, and miles pile up unnoticed. Swimming is gentler and less stressful to the body than most other aerobic activities, so it's a particularly good choice for people who cannot or should not subject their bones and connective tissue to hard, jolting motions. Cycling and rowing, either outdoors, or on stationary machines provide good aerobic workouts if you have the equipment or belong to a fitness centre. There is a range of other choices, such as jogging, skipping, aerobics, in-line or regular roller skating. Focus on one to begin with. Later on, you can vary your workout with other activities.

Switching occasionally from one activity to another helps prevent boredom. And, because different activities work different muscle groups, it allows muscles that are heavily used in one activity an opportunity to recoup the next day as you engage in a different one.

• Ease into it. Regardless of which activity you pick, it is extremely important to get off to a slow start. This helps prevent stress and strain on underused muscles, and gives your heart and lungs a chance to get used to meeting the demands of greater exertion. If you've been sedentary during the previous year, start with no more than ten minutes of your chosen activity a couple of times a week, and instead of giving it all you've got, keep the pace easy and slow.

★ Important ★

Even ten minutes may be too much. If your breathing becomes difficult, or you feel uncomfortable for any reason, it's time to stop even if you've been at it for just a minute or two.

• Build up gradually to at least twenty minutes of brisk aerobic exercise, three or four times a week. Your rate of progress will depend on your weight, your age, your health, and your present fitness level, and it might take months until you are able to manage that much activity. Never mind. Don't rush it along. The idea is gradually to increase the frequency, pace, and duration of your workouts, allowing your body time to adjust.

• Be consistent. Regular activity — even if it's just a few minutes of easy activity per workout — is better for your health, your weight, and your body than more strenuous exercise done only intermittently. To develop consistency in the early stages of a fitness plan, consider gentle exercise for short periods every day. As your endurance increases, and you are able to work out for longer periods of time, you can switch over to more intense, longer-lasting workouts every other day. As you continue with your workouts, you'll become aware of certain changes. You won't feel as fatigued. You'll have more energy for the things in your life that need doing, as well as for the things that you've always wanted to do. You'll experience less stress. Your focus and concentration may improve. Your body will become slimmer, firmer, and take on better proportions. And you'll find that further weight loss — on the New Cabbage Soup Diet, on a diet you customize for yourself, or on any other weight-loss plan you might decide to follow — becomes easier.

Day 8 — Last Words

The New Cabbage Soup Diet has put you on the fast track to quick weight loss. You lost a significant number of pounds and inches on your first time around. From now on, use the New Cabbage Soup Diet periodically to lose more weight more quickly and more easily than you can on any other diet. Just be sure to wait at least fourteen days between cycles. You can use the diet, too, as a quick fix when you hit a plateau on your own custom-tailored long-term weight-loss plan — or any long-term diet you might decide to follow.

Be guided by the Food Guide Pyramid for optimal nutrition between each round of New Cabbage Soup dieting. It will help you maintain your weight loss, and might also result in additional pounds lost.

Incorporate mild to moderate exercise into your life for better health and fitness, easier weight loss, and a greater sense of well-being.

It almost sounds like a prescription for health and happiness, and in many ways it is. With the New Cabbage Soup Diet as your starting point, and the tips, techniques and ideas in this book to help you along, you can be a healthier, happier you.